Whenever my brilliant friend Pastor Craig writes a new book, I take notice. And this newest release does not disappoint. *Winning the War in Your Mind* is a must-read for those who want to identify patterns of unhealthy thinking and what to do about them. So much about life is won or lost in our thoughts. This incredible book is packed full of research, biblical truths, and insightful paradigm shifts that will help you win the daily battles inside your own head. I plan to give this to every member of my family. It's that good!

—Lysa TerKeurst, #1 *New York Times* bestselling author; president, Proverbs 31 Ministries

We can't change what we don't see, and we can't bring to Jesus what we won't take the time to understand. This book is filled with insights from a voice in my life I've trusted for a decade. Craig helps us understand how our minds are wired, why we do what we do, and how we can take our next courageous steps forward in our faith.

—Bob Goff, Sweet Maria Goff's husband

If you're like me and have struggled with anxiety or negative thought patterns, this book is for you. Pastor Craig does an incredible job with relaying how we can change our thinking so that God can transform our lives. The best part is that he uses psychology *and* the Word to bring us truths. This book will show you how to envision your new life and stop believing the lies of the enemy.

—Sadie Robertson Huff, author, speaker, founder of Live Original

Believing lies robs us of the life God intends for us. Through the scope of Scripture and science, Craig gives us powerful strategies to defeat the lies, change our thinking, and win with God's truth.

—Dave Ramsey, bestselling author and radio host

Your thinking determines your destiny. Whether you think you can or think you can't, you're right. This book will give you tools to renew your mind through the power of God's Word so you can live a passionate, purpose-filled life and fulfill your destiny.

—Christine Caine, bestselling author; founder, A21 and Propel Women

Practical and profound. There are few people more skilled than Pastor Craig Groeschel at taking a theological truth and unweaving the tendrils of confusion to get to the clear, meaningful application. That is why I am so confident that this book will both challenge and lead readers toward fruitful life change. I believe that this topic is essential to the holiness of every believer, so this book is a must-read.

—LOUIE GIGLIO, PASTOR, PASSION CITY CHURCH;
FOUNDER, PASSION CONFERENCES; AUTHOR, *DON'T
GIVE THE ENEMY A SEAT AT YOUR TABLE*

Since childhood, I've known that the difference between successful and unsuccessful people is in the way they think. It's a lesson my father taught me, and it has guided me to this day. In his new book, my friend Craig Groeschel brings both science and biblical wisdom to bear on the process of thinking, and shows you how you can change your thinking in order to change your life.

—JOHN C. MAXWELL, FOUNDER, THE
MAXWELL LEADERSHIP ENTERPRISE

It's time to step out of old ways of thinking and start heading toward the life you could be living, a life in which your thoughts no longer control you. I've personally needed these lessons from my friend Craig Groeschel, and I'm so glad he's sharing them with you in his new book.

—STEVEN FURTICK, PASTOR, ELEVATION CHURCH;
NEW YORK TIMES BESTSELLING AUTHOR

Craig is a bold leader who has committed his life to giving away truth to our generation. He's a worthy guide through this important topic.

—JENNIE ALLEN, AUTHOR, *NEW YORK TIMES* BESTSELLING *GET
OUT OF YOUR HEAD*; FOUNDER AND VISIONARY, IF:GATHERING

Craig has taken his trademark enthusiasm to see people win, coupled it with an understanding of brain science and his ability to communicate God's Word, and put it in this book. As you read these pages, there's a pretty good chance your brain and your heart will do a little dance.

—MICHAEL JR., COMEDIAN, AUTHOR, THOUGHT LEADER

WINNING THE WAR IN YOUR MIND

ALSO BY CRAIG GROESCHEL

Altar Ego: Becoming Who God Says You Are

Chazown: Discover and Pursue God's Purpose for Your Life

*The Christian Atheist: Believing in God
but Living as If He Doesn't Exist*

Daily Power: 365 Days of Fuel for Your Soul

*Dangerous Prayers: Because Following Jesus
Was Never Meant to Be Safe*

Dare to Drop the Pose (previously titled *Confessions of a Pastor*)

Divine Direction: Seven Decisions That Will Change Your Life

Fight: Winning the Battles That Matter Most

*From This Day Forward: Five Commitments to Fail-
Proof Your Marriage* (with Amy Groeschel)

Hope in the Dark: Believing God Is Good When Life Is Not

It: How Churches and Leaders Can Get It and Keep It

*Liking Jesus: Intimacy and Contentment in a Selfie-
Centered World* (previously titled *#Struggles*)

Love, Sex, and Happily Ever After (previously
titled *Going All the Way*)

Soul Detox: Clean Living in a Contaminated World

Weird: Because Normal Isn't Working

What Is God Really Like? (general editor)

CRAIG GROESCHEL

WINNING THE WAR

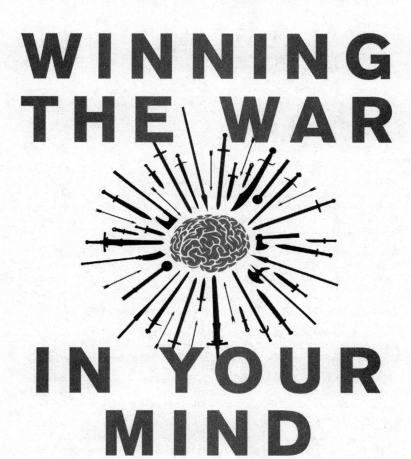

IN YOUR
MIND

CHANGE YOUR THINKING,
CHANGE YOUR LIFE

ZONDERVAN
BOOKS

ZONDERVAN BOOKS

Winning the War in Your Mind
Copyright © 2021 by Craig Groeschel

Requests for information should be addressed to:
Zondervan, 3900 Sparks Dr. SE, Grand Rapids, Michigan 49546

Zondervan titles may be purchased in bulk for educational, business, fundraising, or sales promotional use. For information, please email SpecialMarkets@Zondervan.com.

ISBN 978-0-310-36272-2 (hardcover)
ISBN 978-0-310-36354-5 (international trade paper edition)
ISBN 978-0-310-36274-6 (audio)
ISBN 978-0-310-36273-9 (ebook)

Craig Groeschel is represented by Thomas J. Winters of Winters & King, Inc., Tulsa, Oklahoma.

Cover design: Spencer Fuller | Faceout Studio
Cover illustrations: Shutterstock
Author photo: Life.Church
Interior design: Denise Froehlich

Printed in the United States of America

20 21 22 23 24 25 /LSC/ 10 9 8 7 6 5 4 3 2 1

This book is dedicated to my dad.
You live with the most positive
attitude of anyone I've known.
Thank you for always fighting to find the good
and for inspiring me to change my thinking.
I'm proud you are my dad.

CONTENTS

Introduction: Where Are Your Thoughts Taking You? 1

PART 1: THE REPLACEMENT PRINCIPLE
Remove the Lies, Replace with Truth

1. Perception Is Reality 7
   Exercise 1: Your Thought Audit 20
2. Becoming a Thought Warrior .27
   Exercise 2: Identifying the Lies You Believe 38
3. Old Lies, New Truth 41
   Exercise 3: Declaring Truth 57

PART 2: THE REWIRE PRINCIPLE
Rewire Your Brain, Renew Your Mind

4. Crossed Wires and Circular Ruts 63
   Exercise 4: Recognizing Your Ruts 80
5. Creating a Trench of Truth 83
   Exercise 5: Digging Trenches of Truth 98
6. Rumination and Renewal 101
   Exercise 6: Learning to Ruminate 111

PART 3: THE REFRAME PRINCIPLE
Reframe Your Mind, Restore Your Perspective

7. Lenses and Filters 115
    Exercise 7: Cognitive Bias, Control, and Reframing .124
8. What God Didn't Do. 127
    Exercise 8: Unanswered Prayers 134
9. Collateral Goodness 135
    Exercise 9: Your Collateral Goodness 146

PART 4: THE REJOICE PRINCIPLE
Revive Your Soul, Reclaim Your Life

10. Problems, Panic, and Presence 151
     Exercise 10: When You've Had Enough 167
11. The Perspective of Praise 169
     Exercise 11: Your God Box. 186
12. Look Through, Not At. 187
     Exercise 12: Evaluating What's Right. 198

Conclusion: Choosing to Win the War. 201

Afterword by Amy Groeschel 209
Appendix: Bible Verses for Winning the War 213
Acknowledgments 233
Notes 235

WHERE ARE YOUR
THOUGHTS TAKING YOU?

OUR LIVES ARE ALWAYS MOVING IN THE DIRECTION OF OUR strongest thoughts. What we think shapes who we are.

So you might read that and think I'm being an overly dramatic preacher using hyperbole to get your attention. But this is no exaggeration. Our lives do follow the direction of our thoughts. The better we grasp that truth, the better equipped we'll be to change the trajectory of our lives. But don't take my word for it. Both the Bible and modern science provide evidence that this is true. So throughout this book, we'll unpack both Scripture and what we've learned from scientific research. Here's a brief example of both:

In Philippians 4:8–9, the apostle Paul writes, "Finally, brothers and sisters, whatever is true, whatever is noble, whatever is right, whatever is pure, whatever is lovely, whatever is admirable—if anything is excellent or praiseworthy—think about such things. Whatever you have learned or received or heard from me, or seen in me—put it into practice. And the God of peace will be with you."

In these three sentences Paul moves from

- thought ("think about such things") to
- action ("put it into practice") to
- experience ("the God of peace will be with you").

Paul tells us that our thoughts shape our lives.

In recent years, an entire discipline of modern psychology has developed called cognitive behavioral therapy. This breakthrough teaching reveals that many problems, from eating disorders to relational challenges, addictions, and even some forms of depression and anxiety, are rooted in faulty and negative patterns of thinking.[1] Treating those problems begins with changing that thinking.

I don't know about you, but when the Bible and modern psychology say the same thing, I want to know more.

TIME TO CHANGE YOUR MIND?

In ten years, we will each look in the mirror, and someone will stare back. That person will be shaped by the thoughts of today.

The life we have is a reflection of what we think.

That's a crazy thought, right? What we think will determine who we become tomorrow. And even crazier, we probably don't even realize that's happening! We don't think about the power of our thoughts, which only makes them that much more powerful. But God made us this way. What science is demonstrating today is what God told us through Solomon almost three thousand years ago: "For as he thinks in his heart, so is he" (Prov. 23:7 NKJV).

So if both the Bible and modern science teach us that our lives are moving in the direction of our strongest thoughts, then we need to ask ourselves, "Do I like the direction my thoughts are taking me?"

If your answer is no, then maybe it's time to change your thinking. Decide to change your mind so God can change your life. If you are sick and tired of being sick and tired, of having your life poisoned by toxic thoughts, of being held hostage by those inner voices, I want to encourage you to keep reading and stay open. Whether or not you consider yourself a Christian, I promise there are truths in these pages that will work if you put in some effort to apply them.

As we walk through this important topic together, I want to show you how you can change your thinking *and* transform your life.

In part 1, we'll examine the battle for your mind and how you're really not alone with your thoughts.

In part 2, you'll learn how your brain works and see how to rewire it.

In part 3, you'll discover how to reframe your thinking and redesign your mind around new thoughts.

And in part 4, you'll become equipped to identify your mental triggers and to overcome them through prayer and praise.

Following each chapter, you'll find an exercise that will lead toward the renewal of your mind.

Then, at the end of the book, we'll envision your new life. You will see how you can live free of anxiety and negativity while also experiencing the joy and peace that come from knowing God and living in his truth.

If you're skeptical, that's okay. Believe me, I get it. We've all tried unsuccessfully to change bad habits and force our runaway trains of thought back onto the right tracks. But this time you're not alone. You are about to discover that God will team up with you to transform your thinking. And I'll be your guide to walk with you as you start this journey.

With God's help, you *can* transform your mind.

You can stop believing the lies that hold you back.

You can end the vicious cycle of thoughts that are destructive to you and others.

You can allow God to renew your mind by saturating you with his unchanging truth.

You can let his thoughts become your thoughts.

With that opportunity, let's circle back to our opening statement: Our lives are always moving in the direction of our strongest thoughts. What we think will shape who we become.

If you agree with that proposition—and remember, both the Bible and modern science say it's true—then it's time to change your thinking so God can change your life.

PART 1

THE REPLACEMENT PRINCIPLE

Remove the Lies, Replace with Truth

God has not given us a spirit of fear, but of power and of love and of a sound mind.

—2 TIMOTHY 1:7 NKJV

CHAPTER 1

PERCEPTION IS REALITY

MY FRIEND KEVIN SERVED ON OUR CHURCH STAFF AS ONE of our pastors for close to twenty years before retiring. Way back in the early days, our staff used to play a game called capture the flag in our storefront church offices. We occasionally got violent as players tried to seize the flag. But because we were ministers, it was of course holy violence. Eventually, however, two people ended up getting injured, so we had to establish some guidelines.

One of those rules was no attacks before 8:00 a.m. I tend to get to work early, and one day as I showed up around 7:00 and began walking to my office, my Spidey sense went off. Something wasn't right. Suspecting a threat, I threw open a closet door to find Pastor Kevin hiding. I don't know if he had spent the entire night in there, but his plan was to wait patiently for a surprise attack at go time.

But thanks to my superhero ability to detect danger, I thwarted his plan. I was so excited that I slammed the door shut, wedged my foot against the bottom, and yelled triumphantly, "You're going to spend the day in that closet, Kevin!"

I grabbed a chair to secure my prisoner. Chuckling maniacally, I said, "I'm putting a chair under the doorknob!" But no matter how hard I tried, I couldn't get a chair to fit. And because I couldn't move my foot from the door, there was nothing I could do to lock Kevin in the closet. Fortunately for me, I realized he didn't know that. He believed me. So with all the fake confidence I could muster, I sold it. "There's now a chair under the doorknob, Kevin. You can't get out!" Yes, I lied, but I'm a pastor, so it was holy lying.

Well, what did Kevin do? More like what did he *not* do. He never tried to open the door! He just believed my lie.

Kevin started shouting, "Lemme out! Lemme out! Please, lemme out! I don't want to spend the day in here. Lemme out!"

I couldn't stop laughing. Because the door was unlocked. All he had to do was turn the handle and push, and he would be free. But he just stayed in the closet.

I had a premarital counseling appointment at 8:00, so I went to my office to meet with the soon-to-be-married couple. At about 8:20, I heard something in the ceiling above me. Then I heard the noise again. It was Kevin. He had scaled the shelves in the closet and gotten up into the ceiling tiles, trying to find a way out.

When a ceiling tile suddenly poked out, I saw Kevin's eyes glaring down at me. I asked the couple to forgive the intrusion, then looked up and jokingly said, "If you wait until I'm finished with this meeting, I'll call the fire department and see if they can get you down. If not, you're spending the rest of your life in that ceiling!" The couple I was counseling faced a dilemma: should they laugh or pray for the guy stuck above us?

Out of respect for them, Kevin waited. The whole time, the closet door was unlocked.

I wonder if you feel locked up or taken captive. If so, have you considered that you might be trapped in a self-made prison? You may feel held back from living the life you want to live, not experiencing the relationship you want with God, with little to no hope for the future, but are you? If you think you're trapped, if you believe there's a lock on the door, you've bought into a lie. And it is the lie, nothing else, that is holding you back. Yet if you identify that lie, then you can remove it. You can replace it with the truth and be free. Your liberation is a simple two-step process:

- Remove the lie.
- Replace it with truth.

But the struggle in this process is very real and very hard, and it can feel like a war is being fought in your life. Because that's exactly what is happening.

THE BATTLE FOR YOUR MIND

In the eighties, we were taught that love is a battlefield. Thank you, Pat Benatar! If you're a bit younger, you learned the same lesson from Jordin Sparks. If you are even younger, you know Battlefield as a series of video games.

But no, your *mind* is a battlefield, and the battle for your life is always won or lost in your mind.

Picture a battle with two opposing sides. Now imagine that the people on one side don't realize they're involved in a battle. The enemy is attacking and taking them out, picking them off one by one, but they are oblivious.

Hard to imagine because it's just too absurd? I agree. But every day, you are engaged in a battle; are you aware of it? You may not recognize the battle you're in while it's wreaking havoc in your life. Ever wonder why you can't shake a habit? Why you feel like you can't connect with God? Why you lose your temper so easily? Why you too often make bad decisions? Why you and your spouse fight so much? Why you're consumed with worry, fear, and negativity?

There is a reason why. Your mind is a war zone, and you are under attack. It's critical that you become aware of the fight. You cannot change what you do not confront. If you ignore the battle, you lose the battle. The apostle Paul made this truth clear: "We are not fighting against flesh-and-blood enemies, but against evil rulers and authorities of the unseen world, against mighty powers in this dark world, and against evil spirits in the heavenly places" (Eph. 6:12 NLT).

> **YOU CANNOT CHANGE WHAT YOU DO NOT CONFRONT.**

Your adversary is not your boss, spouse, child, ex, or neighbor with the demonic dog that is always barking. You may not realize it, but the one you are fighting against is your spiritual enemy, the devil. Sound too extreme? That's exactly what your enemy wants.

There is an old saying that goes, "The greatest trick the devil ever pulled was convincing the world he doesn't exist." Satan doesn't want you to believe in him, so he works subtly. He knows that if you ignore him, he can invade your mind with impunity. He can plant seeds of doubt, confusion, worry, depression, and anxiety that will continue to grow.

Satan is your unseen enemy whose mission is to "steal and kill and destroy" (John 10:10), stop you (1 Thess. 2:18), and devour you (1 Peter 5:8). Satan despises you with more hatred than you can imagine. He wants to keep you from God and from the life God has for you. He wants to keep you from intimate relationships with those you love most. He wants to rob you of inner joy and abiding peace. He wants to strip you of the fulfillment you could have in knowing you are making a difference with your life.

So how does he do this?

Simple. He lies. Just like I lied to Kevin about the locked door. Satan is a deceiver, and his strategy to defeat you is to persuade you to believe his lies. Jesus warned us, "There is no truth in him. When he lies, he speaks his native language, for he is a liar and the father of lies" (John 8:44). I think it's interesting that the only time Satan is called a creator, a father, is here in connection to lies.

Understand this: Satan is your enemy, and every day he is prowling around (1 Peter 5:8), watching you, looking for a place where you might believe a lie.

If you succeed at something, maybe he can convince you that you don't need God. If you fail, he'll try to brainwash you into thinking you'll always be a failure.

You have a great first date? He'll suggest romance is the only thing that will make you happy. First date was a disaster? He'll whisper that you'll never have anyone love you for who you are.

If you do a nice thing for a difficult person, he'll murmur that you're a pretty great person yourself and really don't need God's grace. If instead you speak harshly to someone, he'll whisper that you're an awful, hateful person whom God could never love.

If you're trying to stay away from porn, he will tell you everyone else is doing it. If you give in to porn, he'll make you feel like you're the only person sick enough to do such a disgusting thing.

Satan is conniving and trying to lock you in a prison of lies.

But you are not his prisoner of war, unless you choose to be. Those days can be over. That's your call.

AS IF A LIE WERE TRUE

For centuries people believed the world was flat. (Some still do. Don't believe me? Google it. You'll find there are "Flat Earthers" today.) Because they believed the wrong idea, it impacted their lives as if it were true. People would not venture too far out in the ocean for fear they might sail off the edge. Why? Once again, a lie believed as truth will affect your life as if it were true.

Growing up, a lot of us were told that going swimming right after eating wasn't safe. Our parents made us wait thirty minutes after a meal to get in the pool. The only problem is that it's not dangerous to swim after eating. That was and is a lie. Right now you may be thinking, *No, I'm pretty sure that's true.* But it isn't! Yet we believed it, so the lie affected our lives as if it were true.

Missing some swimming time isn't a big deal, but what if you believe significant lies that have serious implications? What if you buy into the lie that you'll never be good enough? Or that you made too many mistakes? Or that God doesn't really care about you? Or that you'll never be able to stop doing what you don't want to do?

One more time, because this point is crucial: a lie believed as truth will affect your life as if it were true.

There is a specific lie I have believed as long as I can remember. Living as if that were true has been one of the biggest limiting forces in my life. For years my strongest thoughts have always been about my shortcomings. I have always felt inadequate. No matter what anyone else said, my inner voice always screamed, *No matter how hard you try, you'll never measure up.*

Why did I feel that way? Frankly, I'm not sure; I have never not felt that way. It seems self-doubt comes naturally to me, but at the same time I could give you a resume proving why I should feel that way.

Essentially, I was living a faithless life.

As I type these words about how we can control our thought life, my mind is racing. As the psalmist often wrote (Ps. 42:5, for example), I am wrestling with my thoughts. I am battling feelings of overwhelming anxiety because I have said yes to too many things and overcommitted myself again.

Yes, my mind is out of control. I wish I could tell you I'm full of faith as I write this first chapter of the book, but my thoughts are full of fear.

But then I come back to what I know is true. And what is true is the point of this book.

I swat at the swarm of thoughts flitting around my head and remember that I am not a victim of my own mind. I have power over my thoughts. I am not captive to them. With God's help, I can make them captive to me.

While I know those truths, at the same time the reality is that I am a struggling thought warrior who has battled insecurity, negativity, fear, and anxiety most of my life.

Midway through college, something dramatic happened to me. Jesus changed my life. By God's grace, he found me and saved me.

Soon I was being so transformed by my relationship with Christ that, while still very new in my faith, I sensed God calling me to be a pastor. (Way before pastors could wear cool shoes and have more Instagram followers than church members.)

As God was building my faith, I felt him telling me I could make a difference in the world through his church. All my childhood insecurities and teenage self-doubts were being eclipsed by glimpses of hope. What do I mean? Well, here's a little backstory for context:

When I was growing up, my family couldn't afford name-brand clothes, so my mother bought used Izod socks at garage sales, cut the alligators out, and sewed them on my generic shirts.

I felt fake.

In second grade I discovered I was color-blind. Not only could

I not match my fake Izod shirts to my no-name pants, but I would never see the beauty of this world as others could.

I felt defective.

In a spelling bee with my classmates, I misspelled Mississippi. We had learned a song teaching us how to spell the word. And every time an *i* appears, there's only one of them and two of everything else. How could I possibly misspell Mississippi?

I felt stupid.

In fifth grade a girl named Tiffany dumped me for a guy named Brian. Her reason? Brian had a motorcycle. I only had a moped. (Yes, twelve-year-olds in my small town drove motorcycles and mopeds.) Tiffany said I was Richie Cunningham and she wanted the Fonz. (If you're too young to remember *Happy Days*, then think of it like she said I was Screech and she wanted Zack Morris.)

I felt lame.

My father played minor league baseball. He was a professional athlete, and I wasn't sure if I could even play in college.

I felt inadequate.

These isolated events, along with many others, formed my perception of myself into the reality I would carry into my newfound faith as a young adult.

I felt I wasn't good enough.

So I learned to play it safe and avoid risks at all costs. I felt that, given any opportunity, I would fail. I quietly came to define success as just not failing.

Chances are good you have your own set of lies holding you back. The lies nearly derailed my call to ministry.

FOR NOW, IT'S A NO

Only weeks after putting my faith in Jesus, I tried to teach my first Bible study to a group of young guys in a little church in Ada, Oklahoma. Afterward the leader of the youth group said, "Well, I guess teaching the Bible is not your gift, is it?"

Three years later I finally got up the nerve to try teaching the Bible again, after being asked to preach my first sermon. After the service, as I stood at the door saying goodbye to church members, an older gentleman looked at me with a raised brow and remarked, "Nice try." Nice try?!

The next lady in line asked if I had any other skills besides being a preacher and then made a weak attempt to encourage me to keep my options open. Seriously, that really happened. I had to fight off the temptation to run and hide in the church baptistry. And yes, full immersion!

Despite yet another setback, still believing God's call, I continued my journey toward full-time vocational ministry by going to seminary following college and marriage. About halfway through seminary, the day finally came when I stood before a group of spiritual leaders as a candidate for ordination in our denominational church. With the entire committee looking on, the spokesperson explained to me, "We've chosen not to ordain you. You don't have the gift-mix we see in most pastors. In fact, we are not sure you are called to be a pastor. But feel free to try again next year. But for now, it's a no."

Immediately all those childhood memories met up with my

teenage memories. They all joined forces with the rejections from the church, forming an avalanche of negative thoughts that crashed over me, engulfing me. The voices roared loudly, *You aren't enough! You will never be enough! You will never measure up!*

And then the final verdict was delivered: *You . . . don't . . . have . . . what it takes!*

Driving home in my red Geo Prizm, I felt dejected, embarrassed, confused, and angry. Devastated. *How can I explain to my wife that I didn't make the cut? How can I face my pastor? My friends? My classmates? The church where I serve?* The tears flowed as every possible negative thought played on repeat.

But then a strange thing happened.

Suddenly a different voice interrupted the others. God spoke. He spoke to *me*. While not audible, the words somehow seemed louder than any physical voice I had ever heard.

In that moment, my heavenly Father said, "You are not who others say you are. You are who *I* say you are. And I say you are called to ministry."

While that was of course one of the most powerful moments of my life and a massive turning point, I wasn't suddenly healed of my negative think-

> **" YOU ARE NOT WHO OTHERS SAY YOU ARE. YOU ARE WHO *I* SAY YOU ARE. "**

ing or delivered from believing every lie I'd told myself while growing up. The patterns were still there. The consequences were still ingrained. But I began to realize God had a very different way for me to think and a much healthier way for me to think of myself. I realized he was offering me a choice of whether to continue to believe my lies or accept his truth about me.

That's the beauty of allowing God to master our minds: he gives us a new path, a new way to think, but we have to get on board, agree, and cooperate with him.

LIE DETECTION

How about you? What negative messages did you take away from your childhood?

What unhealthy and destructive conclusions have you come to believe about yourself and your place in the world?

Satan's strategy to win the battle for your mind is getting you to believe lies. If you believe a lie, it will hold you back from doing what God's calling you to do.

The lie will keep you living in shame from the past, when God wants to set you free for a better future.

The lie will keep you from living with joy and freedom and confine you to a less-than existence.

When legendary magician Harry Houdini came into a town to do his show, he often went to the local jail, gathering a crowd of people along the way. To get buzz going about his upcoming performance, he asked the jailer to lock him in a cell. Time after time, jail after jail, town after town, Houdini escaped within minutes.

But one jailer had heard that Houdini was coming, and the jailer was ready. When Houdini closed the cell door, the jailer put the key in the lock and secretly turned it in the wrong direction. He then removed the key, and everyone watched as Houdini struggled to escape—by unknowingly locking himself in repeatedly. Finally, in frustration, Houdini admitted he could not escape. The jailer then revealed his deception. Houdini had believed a lie, and the lie had held him captive.

Living your life by a lie is a lot like believing the door is locked when it isn't. On the other side is freedom. But you first have to commit to some personal lie detection to experience the abundant life Jesus came and died to give you. That leads us to our first exercise.

—— EXERCISE 1 ——
YOUR THOUGHT AUDIT

DO YOU EVER FIND YOURSELF THINKING THINGS LIKE:

- I just can't change. Even if I try, I'll always be stuck.
- I can never get out of debt. No matter what I do, I'll always struggle financially.
- No one really loves me. And if they knew the real me, they'd definitely not want to be in my life.
- I'm not good at relationships. When we start to grow closer, I always do something to mess things up.
- People in my family struggle with their weight. I'll never like my body.
- I can't get close to God. I'm sure it's my fault. There must be something about me that keeps me from experiencing God like others do.
- When I look at what others post on social media, I feel like my life sucks.

If you think you can't do something, you probably won't. If, on the other hand, you think you can, odds are you will. The same is true with your problems. If you dwell on them, they will overwhelm you. But if you look for solutions, you will find some.

If you feel like a victim, you'll think like a victim, and the direction of your life could be one of misery. But if you believe that by the power of Christ you can overcome, then with his help you can. Consider this:

- Who you are today is a result of your thoughts in the past.
- Who you become in the future will reflect what you think about today.

Whether it's self-doubts or worrying or responding poorly to a bad day or a tough season in life, we all wrestle with negative thoughts that try to hijack our emotions and decisions.

The goal of this exercise is to give you the opportunity to think about what you think about.

Let's conduct a thought audit. Hit pause for a moment and prepare your mind. Focus on your honest answers. This could begin the process of you changing your mind. There are two parts to this exercise.

PART 1: INVENTORY

As you go through a normal day, take stock of your thoughts. Write them down, type them into the notes on your phone, or record them in your voice memo app to transcribe later. Trust me, if you really want to change, you need to invest the time to figure out what you are regularly thinking. Be honest. Don't lie to yourself about the lies you tell yourself.

Evaluate the factors consistent in your day. Are you more negative in the morning but usually level out by the end of your workday? Or the opposite? Do you tend to bring negative thinking home with you? Or do you manage to leave it at work? Consider all the dynamics and patterns of your day. Pray and ask God to reveal anything he wants you to see and understand in how you think.

Once you see your thoughts in black and white, you can begin to work on your thought life. Jesus said the truth sets us free, but first we must reveal the truth.

PART 2: AUDIT

Here are twenty questions to help you analyze what you regularly think. I've broken down the questions into two categories: defense (protection from the Enemy) and offense (growth toward God). Write down your honest answers. When you're done, compare your defense and offense. This evaluation will help you see your thoughts and work on real change.

On a typical day:

DEFENSE:

- **Are my thoughts tearing me down?**

- Do I think worried thoughts?

- Does my self-talk cause me to shrink back in fear?

- Do my thoughts cause me to keep people at a distance?

- Are my unhealthy thoughts keeping me from the life I want?

- Are my unhealthy thoughts keeping me from the life God wants for me?

- Are my thoughts negative, toxic, or self-deprecating?

- Does my inner voice tell me I'm helpless or that life is hopeless?

- Do I find myself skeptical of others?

- Do I lean toward imagining worst-case scenarios?

OFFENSE:

- Are my thoughts building me up?

- Do I think peaceful thoughts?

- Does my self-talk inspire me to take faith risks?

- Do my thoughts help me get closer to others?

- Do my thoughts reflect my faith?

- Are my thoughts God-honoring?

- Do my thoughts reflect my hope in Christ?

- Do they inspire me to believe I can make a difference in the world?

- Do they equip me to become more like Jesus?

- **Do my thoughts connect to the vision God has for my life?**

Remember, the goal is to think about what you think about. You can use this information as we move forward, to help you take practical steps in winning the battle in your mind. As we continue, we will get to some answers that deal with the truth you have revealed in this exercise. Be encouraged. You are one step closer to changing your thinking and believing what God says about you.

CHAPTER 2

BECOMING A THOUGHT WARRIOR

THE PROFESSOR GUIDING US IN THE ADVANCED THOUGHT-ology course we are about to take will be the apostle Paul. His writings will teach us the biblical way to win the battle in our minds.

Incredible as it is to consider, Paul wrote some of his teachings while in prison. And yes, his door was actually locked. Yet even though his body was behind bars, Paul's mind was still free. How? He had taken his thoughts captive long before he entered a jail cell. He knew two truths that we also need to know:

1. The battle for your life is won or lost in your mind.
2. Your thoughts *will* control you, so you have to control your thoughts.

Paul had not always been a thought warrior. Check out how he described himself in Romans 7:15–24:

I do not understand what I do. For what I want to do I do not do, but what I hate I do. And if I do what I do not want to do, I agree that the law is good. As it is, it is no longer I myself who do it, but it is sin living in me. For I know that good itself does not dwell in me, that is, in my sinful nature. For I have the desire to do what is good, but I cannot carry it out. For I do not do the good I want to do, but the evil I do not want to do—this I keep on doing. Now if I do what I do not want to do, it is no longer I who do it, but it is sin living in me that does it.

So I find this law at work: Although I want to do good, evil is right there with me. For in my inner being I delight in God's law; but I see another law at work in me, waging war against the law of my mind and making me a prisoner of the law of sin at work within me. What a wretched man I am!

That does not sound like a guy who has mastered his thoughts. While we all get what he is saying, that just sounds a little crazy. But check out how Paul describes himself in Philippians 4:12: "I have learned the secret of being content in any and every situation." Now, that does sound like a guy who has mastered his thoughts.

Paul's change encourages me. Because my thought life can be crazy. My mind can run out of control. I despair. I obsess. I can be confused. Sometimes I feel overwhelmed. It's like I'm in a confrontation with myself, and I'm losing.

Yet honestly, we can all be a bit crazy, right? You try not to worry, but you do. You tell yourself to be positive, but you aren't. Like Paul said, "What I want to do I do not do." The daily battle is so frustrating!

But Paul mastered his mind. He said he had learned a secret. So that means we can too.

How did he win the battle for his mind? How can we? Paul also wrote, "Though we live in the world, we do not wage war as the world does. The weapons we fight with are not the weapons of the world. On the contrary, they have divine power to demolish strongholds. We demolish arguments and every pretension that sets itself up against the knowledge of God, and we take captive every thought to make it obedient to Christ" (2 Cor. 10:3–5).

Notice that Paul used *we* in his statements. Those in a relationship with Christ can experience this change. Let's break down his words and see how the application can transform our lives.

ONE, TWO, THREE, FOUR, I DECLARE A WAR

Remember thumb wrestling as a kid? Well, there is a World Thumb Wrestling Championship held in the United Kingdom each year. I know. I found that hard to believe as well.

Two big, jacked, tattooed guys with names like Under the Thumb and Jack the Gripper stare menacingly at each other. You know they mean business. But when they say, "One, two, three, four, I declare a thumb war," that's when I lose interest. Two guys battling with their thumbs in a little professional thumb wrestling ring just doesn't keep my attention.

You and I, however, are actually in a war. I know. I can find it hard to believe too. Because most days, it just doesn't feel that way. Life just seems normal.

But we are in a war. One that has less to do with our thumbs and everything to do with what's above our eyebrows.

I don't know about you, but I have never glared at the devil and said with him, "One, two, three, four, I declare a spiritual war." But maybe it's time? Forget the thumbs. Declare war.

Yet Paul said, "We do not wage war as the world does" (2 Cor. 10:3).

The problem is that many Christians don't wage war at all. Satan is assaulting us with evil. He's delivering blows of deception and bombarding us with lies. But we can be oblivious to the attacks.

As a result, our lives are not what we want, and we numb ourselves to reality. We long for more but settle for less. We keep ourselves too busy and distracted. We buy things, attempting to impress people and fill some mysterious, inner, endless void. We scroll mindlessly on social media, feeling left out, left behind, and unimportant as we compare our dull lives with everyone else's highlight reels. We do our best to pretend we are happy, while a war rages around us. And as a result, we are losing battle after battle.

You may recall from history class that the United States took a while to engage in World War II. We spent the first years maintaining a neutral position. We believed that because the war was "over there," it wasn't impacting our lives. Eventually it became clear that Hitler and the Axis powers would not stop, and the freedom of the entire world was hanging in the balance. When the Japanese bombed our naval base at Pearl Harbor, that provocation was the final straw.

Finally, the U.S. entered the war. On D-Day, we joined with other Allied forces as 150,000 troops stormed the beaches of Normandy. The Germans had set about four million land mines to protect the beach from such an invasion. They also rained down gunfire on our men. The sacrifices that day were enormous. Thousands of lives were lost. But the engagement was necessary because there was no other way to defeat evil.

To win the battle for our minds, we must engage, because there is no other way for us to defeat evil. The days of being neutral must be over.

A few years ago, I began to feel stuck. My thoughts were out of control. I would work on my message for the church,

> **TO WIN THE BATTLE FOR OUR MINDS, WE MUST ENGAGE, BECAUSE THERE IS NO OTHER WAY FOR US TO DEFEAT EVIL.**

thinking, *Last week's message wasn't good enough, and this one won't be either. I just don't have what it takes. I'm not good enough. I'm not sure I can keep this up. I don't know why people even come to this church.*

If I poured more energy into being a better pastor, I felt like I was failing as a husband and dad. If I gave my best to my family, I was sure I was letting God down and failing the people in my church. Inside my mind, land mines were everywhere and I was dodging bullets.

My strongest thoughts were centered on my weakness, and I knew they were leading me to a place I did not want to go. Finally, I decided I'd had enough. I had to do something. It was time to win the battle for my mind.

One, two, three, four, I declare a thought war.

For about two years, my mind was my number one priority of prayer. I read so many books on the topic that I lost count. I also received counseling from a psychologist and confided in trusted friends and mentors.

I discovered and started using tools that allowed me to practice two disciplines: retrain my thought patterns and reorient my trajectory.

Bottom line, I knew that if I ignored the battle any longer, I'd lose it.

So I changed my thinking, and that decision changed my life.

DESTROYING THE STRONGHOLD

The lies we believe and base our lives upon are strongholds. Paul said, "The weapons we fight with . . . have divine power to demolish strongholds" (2 Cor. 10:4). So we need to demolish those lies that harm us.

The word stronghold is translated from the Greek word *ochuroma*, which means "to fortify." In ancient times, a stronghold was a building, a fortress built on top of the highest peak in the city. This citadel was surrounded by a reinforced wall up to twenty feet thick.

In times of war, if the city was attacked, the stronghold was often seen as unapproachable and impenetrable. Political leaders were hidden there so they wouldn't be captured or killed.

Paul compared the lies we believe to those fortresses. Like the walls of the strongholds, our lies have been reinforced over and over to become bigger and stronger. We have believed them for so long, they have become a part of us. We believe our walls protect us. We think they are impenetrable. And yet they often keep the truth unapproachable to us.

We have mental and emotional strongholds—the lies that have a "strong hold" on us.

I told you before about my belief that I could never be enough—not good enough, smart enough, or successful enough. I thought I had to prove I was worthy. You may have read that and thought, *But Craig, you're a pastor. You know the Bible. God tells us that we don't need to be enough. Jesus was enough for us. Craig, you know that God loves you and that's all that matters.* Yes, you would be right. I did know that. I taught that. But deep down I felt like that truth applied to everyone but me.

Knowing those truths was not enough to penetrate the walls of my stronghold. My stronghold kept the truth unapproachable. I still believed the lie that I was not worthy and had to prove myself, and that lie affected my life as if it were true. Yes, even as a pastor who taught others that very truth.

Solomon gave us some very wise counsel to apply to this

battle: "One who is wise can go up against the city of the mighty and pull down the stronghold in which they trust" (Prov. 21:22).

If you are in a war and attack a city, make sure you take down the stronghold. If you don't take the more difficult action of bringing it down, the city will reestablish itself. The leaders are hiding inside the walls, still very much alive.

So you have to bring down the stronghold.

Our word demolish is translated from the Greek word *kathaireo*, which means "destruction requiring massive power." The word also means "to lower with violence"—to bring something down with brute strength, as with a wrecking ball.

Regardless of our perceived strength, you and I do not have massive, wrecking-ball power. But God does, and he has made it available to us.

Yet again Paul taught us the concept: "I also pray that you will understand the incredible greatness of God's power for us who believe him. This is the same mighty power that raised Christ from the dead" (Eph. 1:19–20 NLT).

That's incredible! The same power that raised Jesus from the dead is available to you and me.

Wow! Let that truth sink in.

You have supernatural, resurrection, roll-the-stone-away power at hand to change your mind, transform your thoughts, and win the war. If God's power can take Jesus from death to life, then whatever you need can be done for you too. That's the kind of massive power God is offering you. Isn't that encouraging? You've got astonishing power to help you.

DON'T GIVE UP, LOOK UP

What's your stronghold?

What lie is holding you hostage?

What mistruth keeps you from taking a step of faith?

What wrong thought pattern robs you of living a life of freedom and joy?

Know this: You cannot defeat what you cannot define. You have to identify the lie that has become a stronghold for you. You must realize the negative impact it's had on you and others.

Do you see how you have become a prisoner of deception, locked up by a lie you believe is true? If you are going to change your life, you have to change your thinking. Demolish your strongholds.

> **" YOU CANNOT DEFEAT WHAT YOU CANNOT DEFINE. "**

If you want to truly change your life, you cannot just change your behavior. Even if you change your actions for a while, the original issue will just reestablish itself. That's why Christianity has never been about behavior modification; it's about life transformation.

We've all experienced that frustration, right? We make a New Year's resolution or some commitment to start or stop doing something. Lose weight, quit smoking, pray more, stop yelling at the kids. Well, for a few weeks it seems to work, and then we go right back to doing what we always do. Why? We haven't gotten to the root of the problem: the lie we believe.

Addressing the problem is attacking the city. Identifying and destroying the lie is pulling down the stronghold. Both are necessary to win the war.

To do both and experience success, we need God's power. We cannot have victory without his strength and support.

I have good news that might sound like bad news at first. You ready?

You don't have what it takes to win the war. Neither do I.

You know it because you've tried. You've tried to change your thinking, tried to change your life. You've done everything you can, but you always end up back in the same place. You keep doing what you don't want to do and not doing what you want to do, just like Paul. You keep falling down and falling short. I get it. Been there, done that.

All the trying and failing and falling can lead to a place where we feel like giving up.

What's the problem? The power you need is a power you don't possess. Relying on your own power is self-help, and self-help goes only skin deep.

You have a devious spiritual enemy. You have reinforced strongholds. What stands against you is formidable. Fighting in your own power is like attacking Godzilla with a flyswatter.

Admitting that you need a power you don't possess is vital, even though it may be difficult. I know it has been for me. If you've been taught to be an independent, self-reliant, pull-yourself-up-by-your-bootstraps individual, confessing you don't have what it takes might feel like weakness. But it's not. It takes real strength to admit, *I can't do this on my own. I need power greater than I possess.*

Once, after a blizzard, I tried to shovel a path to our cars, to get enough snow off our driveway to back them out. In two solid backbreaking hours, I had cleared a pathway big enough for a small squirrel to walk through. Just as my wife was about to call 911 to save me from permanent frostbite damage, a neighbor from down the street drove by on his tractor. Yes, my neighbor drives a tractor. I live in Oklahoma. In a matter of minutes, because of the power he possessed, my helpful neighbor had cleared our entire driveway.

We tend to fight our battles with shovel power. But we need tractor power. We need a power we don't possess. We have to ask for and receive help.

Remember the popular definition of insanity? Keep doing the same thing, expecting different results. If you have tried with everything you have and it hasn't worked, stop. Don't keep doing the same thing. You'll get the same results. If you feel like you just have to admit defeat and stop trying, don't do that either. Because you'll keep living the same life.

Don't give up. Look up.

Look up because you have a gracious, generous God who has the power you need and wants to share it with you.

To bring down your strongholds, it's time to go up. As a child of God, you have access to everything that belongs to your heavenly Father. So look up, go up, and access the power God has that you need to remove lies and replace them with truth. Ask him to show you the lies that you have believed for too long. Tell him you want your mind to be filled with his truths instead of the devil's falsehoods. And then thank him for hearing you.

—— EXERCISE 2 ——

IDENTIFYING THE
LIES YOU BELIEVE

IN THE FIRST EXERCISE, YOU TOOK AN HONEST INVENTORY and made an audit of how you tend to think on a regular basis. In this exercise, we're going to dive deeper and get more specific.

I want to repeat a crucial section of this chapter that needs to be connected to this exercise:

What lie is holding you hostage?

What mistruth keeps you from taking a step of faith?

What wrong thought pattern robs you of living a life of freedom and joy?

Know this: You cannot defeat what you cannot define. You have to identify the lie that has become a stronghold for you. You must realize the negative impact it's had on you and others.

Use these questions to trigger your thoughts; it's now time to define the lies you've been believing, identify the strongholds in your life, and face their negative impact.

Freeing yourself from all distractions, focus on identifying the specific lies you believe. I have given you plenty of examples of lies I've believed and have had to address, both old ones and new ones. Make your statements personal and straightforward, as in, "I believe I am not good enough." Get them out. Write them down.

My lies:

CHAPTER 3

OLD LIES, NEW TRUTH

IF WE ARE GOING TO DEMOLISH OUR STRONGHOLDS, WE have to recognize the power that lies have over us. Think of it this way.

There is a large, shaggy-haired, lumbering dog—let's call him Max—who will not leave the yard. A car drives by. Max loves to chase cars. The thought of grabbing one by the bumper and wrestling the beast into submission makes him drool. Max wants to give chase so badly, but he just sits in the yard.

Then two boys start playing catch in the street. The ball rolls right to the edge of Max's yard. He desperately wants to get the ball and run from the boys. But he doesn't. One of them teases the dog. "What's the matter, Max? Afraid of the ball?" Max wants to bite the brat, but his tormentor is just outside the yard.

A cat walks down the street. Max cannot imagine the nerve of this cat. He knows they are evil and that they are on this earth only to do Satan's work. Max wants to attack, to bring a hailstorm of violence onto this feline's life. Yet he cannot.

Why?

An invisible electric fence lines the perimeter of his yard.

This type of fence puts out a little invisible beam, and when an unsuspecting dog crosses the line—zap! He gets a small jolt of electricity. The first time the dog is confused. He tries to leave the yard again—zap. Another painful little sting. If the dog is stubborn, or just dumb, he might try a third time. After that he's learned his lesson. He knows he will never be able to leave the yard again.

Max's owners have an invisible electric fence.

Actually, Max's owners *used* to have an electric fence. They bought one, set it up, and turned it on. Max was shocked several times. The fence also zapped a neighbor kid who tried to come into their yard to get a stray frisbee. The kid's parents complained, and Max's owners decided to return the electric fence to the store.

Several years have passed since they owned the fence. Even still, Max will not leave the yard. Why? He thinks he can't. He believes he can't. In his mind he is a prisoner, missing out on the life he wants to live. He associates life outside the boundaries of his yard with pain. The magical place where cars can be caught, balls can be stolen, and the evil mission of cats can be thwarted is just out of reach. He has no idea that the only thing keeping him constrained is a lie he believes.

You laugh, but is it possible you may be more like Max than you think?

Are you also a prisoner, missing out on the life you want but believe you can never have? You crave close relationships but are paralyzed by the fear of rejection. You want to try something new but assume you are destined to fail. You long to be debt free and give generously but feel certain that could never be you. You dream of losing weight and exercising but feel resigned to fail yet again. You want to change but think you never can.

Why?

You are constrained by a lie, something that doesn't exist. The Enemy has arranged enough hurtful circumstances, in key places of your life, in which you got just enough jolt—a bit of a shock, a sting of pain to your heart—that you have decided trying even one more time is just not worth the risk. What makes it worse is that the number of places where you have stopped trying is growing ever larger.

As we've discussed, the greatest weapon in Satan's arsenal is the lie. Perhaps his only weapon is the lie. The first glimpse we have of the devil in the Bible, we see him deceiving Adam and Eve in the garden. He created doubt in Eve's mind by asking her,

"Did God really say, 'You must not eat from any tree in the garden'?"

The woman said to the serpent, "We may eat fruit from the trees in the garden, but God did say, 'You must not eat fruit from the tree that is in the middle of the garden, and you must not touch it, or you will die.'"

"You will not certainly die," the serpent said to the woman.

"For God knows that when you eat from it your eyes will be opened, and you will be like God, knowing good and evil."

—GENESIS 3:1–5

What Satan did in the garden back then is the exact same thing he will attempt to do in your life today.

In 2 Corinthians 11:3, our thoughtology professor Paul said, "I am afraid that just as Eve was deceived by the serpent's cunning, your minds may somehow be led astray from your sincere and pure devotion to Christ."

Satan will whisper accusing questions and deceptive statements. He schemes to twist your mind, because if he can, he then

- diverts you from your purpose,
- distracts you from God's voice,
- destroys your potential.

If he can get you to believe a lie, your life will be affected as if that lie were true.

Unfortunately, Satan's lies are easy to believe. Why? Part of the reason is that because of sin, we have a flawed internal lie detector. God warned us:

- "The heart is deceitful above all things and beyond cure" (Jer. 17:9).
- "There is a way that appears to be right, but in the end it leads to death" (Prov. 14:12).

That's definitely the problem, so what's our solution? How do we access God's power to stop Satan's lies? How can we demolish his strongholds in our lives?

If Satan's primary weapon is lies, then our greatest counterweapon is the truth of God's Word. Not just reading the Bible but learning to wield Scripture as a divine weapon. God wants us to view his Word that way. See how Hebrews 4:12 offers a direct solution to the warning of Jeremiah 17:9: "The word of God is alive and active.

> **IF SATAN'S PRIMARY WEAPON IS LIES, THEN OUR GREATEST COUNTERWEAPON IS THE TRUTH OF GOD'S WORD.**

Sharper than any double-edged sword, it penetrates even to dividing soul and spirit, joints and marrow; it judges the thoughts and attitudes of the heart."

In Ephesians 6:17, Paul's legendary armor of God passage, the Word of God is called "the sword of the Spirit." God's Word was the first weapon I learned to use to remove lies and replace them with truth, changing both my thinking and my life. "Do not conform to the pattern of this world, but be transformed by the renewing of your mind" (Rom. 12:2).

The second half of that sentence is in the passive voice, meaning it is not something we do but instead something that is done to us. The good news is that God is ready to renew our minds by leading us to "a knowledge of the truth" (2 Tim. 2:25). Why? So we can "come to [our] senses and escape from the trap of the devil, who has taken [us] captive to do his will" (v. 26). "Then," as Jesus said, "[we] will know the truth, and the truth will set [us] free" (John 8:32).

TURNING THE TABLES

We've been held captive by the lies we believe, so now we are going to take those lies captive. Capturing the lie is not so easy, because first we must realize the lie. How? Here is our three-step process:

1. Identify the problem.
2. Ask probing questions.
3. Pinpoint the lie.

This process can work because while you don't know the lies you believe are lies, you do know that the problems you experience are problems. Problems are easier to identify, so if you're willing to ask some probing questions, you will be able to pinpoint the lies that are holding you captive.

I'll show you how this works with some examples.

Let's say your problem is enormous consumer debt. You are constantly buying the newest and bestest. (Yes, I know *bestest* is not a word.) You go on expensive vacations. You buy a cool car. You rock the latest phone. You drink the hippest coffee. You purchase even hipper clothes. And shoes? You have a different pair of shoes for every day of the month! You keep buying more, drowning yourself financially.

You have identified a problem. Now ask probing questions like:

- Why am I doing this?
- When did this start?

- How does this make me feel?
- Is fear driving this?
- If so, what am I afraid of?
- Is there a certain trigger that prompts this behavior?
- If so, why do I often spend so compulsively?

As you ask your probing questions, pray for God's help to pinpoint the lie at the root of your behavior. Perhaps you'll remember how you grew up poor and your parents were always bemoaning what they didn't have. That gave the devil an opportunity to deceive you into believing the lie, "If I just had better stuff, I'd fit in" or "If I had more, I would be happy." Buying more, newer, bester (also not a word) stuff does not make you happy. Yet you keep spending, because a lie believed as true will affect your life as if it were true.

Perhaps the problem you identify is a self-destructive habit or addiction. Maybe you regularly sit down and eat a half gallon of ice cream. Come home from work every day and immediately pour yourself a drink. Can't relax without the help of pills. Or keep turning to toxic relationships.

That's the problem; now ask probing questions.

- What is driving my behavior?
- What need do I feel this is meeting?
- Does when I do this help me understand why I do it?
- What is different about this habit than others I have been able to quit?

The questions may lead you to the conclusion that a substance you use (is chocolate ice cream a substance?) helps relieve stress and gives you a temporary feeling of peace. You may realize something is just providing a momentary endorphin rush that never ends in a good place.

Your first thought might be, *What's wrong with that?* but I'm guessing you already know. God promises to be our refuge, the one who gives us rest, our peace provider. So who might put the idea in your head that God can't do what he promises and that you need to turn to something other than him instead?

Let's say your questions lead you to detect a theme in your life: you seem to sabotage yourself. You let people walk all over you. You don't get the promotion. You don't even apply for the promotion, because you believe that kind of thing never happens to you. You would love to have a special someone to share your life with, but now you're not even looking, because you are sure you will never find anyone like that, or if you do, they will reject you. Why? Search your feelings.

> " GOD PROMISES TO BE OUR REFUGE, THE ONE WHO GIVES US REST, OUR PEACE PROVIDER. "

You investigate the pattern of self-sabotage, and perhaps you have an epiphany. *I think I'm a victim. I believe I can never win.*

Maybe your problem is that you worry constantly. You are always trying to plan out all the details of your future because you cannot stand not knowing the plan.

Get alone, turn off the phone, pray for help in being honest with yourself, and ask probing questions, such as:

- When did this start?
- Why do I feel this way?
- Why do I insist on being in control when I know, deep down, I'm not?
- What is the real need I'm trying to meet with this wrong thinking?

Then pinpoint the lie. It could be that you believe God can't really be trusted. You need to be in control, because that is your best bet at getting the life you want. You realize that rather than surrendering yourself to God, you are trying to manipulate him to serve your own purposes.

See how this works?

Allow me to show you how this has played out in my life.

I grew up an overachiever. Not because I was gifted but because I worked myself into the ground trying to hide my deficits and compensate for my weaknesses. I believed that if I worked harder than anyone else, I could somehow prove my worth and value.

I entered into full-time ministry as a young, twenty-three-year-old married man. I was also a full-time seminary student. My wife and I started multiplying like rabbits. I worked nonstop. I would go months without taking a single day off. Every day, I was the first one to work and the last one to leave. I went years without taking a real vacation.

For a long time I believed my work ethic was a God-honoring way to live. One evening I was working late at the office again. My daughter Catie called. I promised her I'd be home soon to play with her. Catie replied with sadness, "Daddy, you don't live at home. You live at the office."

As soon as I heard her innocent but honest statement, time stood still. It was hard to breathe. God got my attention through my little girl. I was putting everything that really matters at risk. I realized I had a problem and had to change.

When you identify a problem, what do you do? You ask probing questions.

So I did. I asked. I prayed. I sought help from a therapist.

Eventually I pinpointed the lie: I believed my worth was based on what other people thought of me. The problem was I had become a people pleaser.

I believed a lie, and it affected my life as if it were true.

Have these examples raised some red flags in your life?

Is it time for you to identify a problem?

Ask some probing questions?

Pinpoint a lie? Maybe a few?

Remember, you are in a battle. The battle is for your mind. Your entire life, Satan has been trying to bait you so he can entice you with lies that will capture and imprison you. Now it's time to go on the offensive. Time to get God's help to capture the lie.

ONLY THE TRUTH CAN SET YOU FREE

The battle we're in is especially insidious because it's invisible. We can't see our enemy. We don't realize he's the one leading us to believe the lies (which we probably don't even recognize as lies). But there was one time in history when this battle was not invisible, and that provides clear clues about how to wield God's massive power to demolish enemy-occupied strongholds.

In Matthew 4 we read about Jesus, after his baptism, heading into the desert, where he fasts for forty days and nights. At that time Satan comes to Jesus to tempt him.

Because he knew Jesus had to be hungry, Satan told him to turn stones into bread. Just as he did with Adam and Eve, Satan was trying to get Jesus to do something that wasn't part of God's plan for his life. (That's also what Satan does with you.)

Jesus replied, "It is written: 'Man shall not live on bread alone, but on every word that comes from the mouth of God'" (Matt. 4:4), quoting Deuteronomy 8:3.

Satan realized his first plan failed, so he attacked Jesus from a different angle. (That is also exactly what Satan does with you.) Same method, new try.

The devil took Jesus to the highest point on the temple in Jerusalem and dared him to throw himself off. Satan decided that two can play this game, so he quoted Psalm 91: "It is written: 'He will command his angels concerning you, and they will lift you up in their hands, so that you will not strike your foot against a stone'" (Matt. 4:6). (Yes, Satan knows the Bible too.) He wanted to tempt Jesus to prove he was truly God's Son by trying to force God to show evidence of his love and care.

Jesus stayed on point and simply answered, "Do not put the Lord your God to the test" (Matt. 4:7), quoting Deuteronomy 6:16.

That didn't work either, so Satan tried a different way of

burrowing his way into Jesus' thinking. (Again, that is exactly what Satan does with you.)

He brought Jesus to a tall mountain, showed him the kingdoms of the world, and offered to give it all to him if Jesus would just bow down and worship him.

Jesus had now had enough and commanded, "Away from me, Satan!" He then quoted Deuteronomy 6:13: "For it is written: 'Worship the Lord your God, and serve him only'" (Matt. 4:10).

Shouldn't we take the same approach that Jesus did?

We are going to "take captive every thought to make it obedient to Christ" (2 Cor. 10:5) by using our process to pinpoint the lie, and then we will replace that lie with the truth that sets us free.

Three times, in three separate instances and temptations, Jesus exposed Satan's lie and engaged the truth of God's Word that he had been memorizing since he was a young Jewish boy.

The first tool I learned that renewed my mind and transformed my life was the Replacement Principle: Remove the lies, replace with truth. Once you grasp this tool, this weapon, you can begin to use it regularly to change your mind and your life.

Jesus' clear example, detailed for us in Matthew 4, is why it is essential that we know the Bible. As followers of Christ, we prioritize reading the Bible, listen to Bible teaching, join Bible studies, and get God's Word into our hearts so we can wield the sword against the lies of the Enemy.

Let's see how this could work with the examples we considered earlier.

You identified a problem of overspending. You asked probing questions that led you to expose the lie you believed: "If I had more, then I would be happy."

The next step is to replace that lie with God's truth. "I know what it is to be in need, and I know what it is to have plenty. I have learned the secret of being content in any and every situation, whether well fed or hungry, whether living in plenty or in want. I can do all this through him who gives me strength" (Phil. 4:12–13).

Now write this biblical truth into your own declaration: "I can be content regardless of my circumstances—in plenty or in want—because no matter what I don't have, I know I do have Jesus. That means I can 'rejoice in the Lord always' (Phil. 4:4)."

The problem that plagues you is a self-destructive habit—ice cream, alcohol, pills, bad relationships. You captured the lie: you believe you need whatever it is to help relieve stress and give you peace.

What's the truth? Jesus said, "Come to me, all you who are weary and burdened, and I will give you rest. Take my yoke upon you and learn from me, for I am gentle and humble in heart, and you will find rest for your souls. For my yoke is easy and my burden is light" (Matt. 11:28–30).

Your declaration: "I do need help; I need God's help. What I am using may numb me to my problem but does not help me. God tells me to come to him when I am weary, burdened, or overwhelmed. He tells me to 'cast all [my] anxiety on him because he cares for [me]' (1 Peter 5:7), and he promises to be my 'refuge and strength, an ever-present help in trouble' (Ps. 46:1)."

You get the pattern now, but here are a couple more in a concise template:

Lie: "I'm a victim; nothing good ever happens to me."

Truth: "If God is for us, who can be against us? . . . In all these things we are more than conquerors through him who loved us" (Rom. 8:31, 37).

Declaration: "God tells me that I am not a victim but a victor in Christ. I am an overcomer, and 'I can do all this through him who gives me strength'" (Phil. 4:13).

Lie: "God can't really be trusted. I need to be in control of my own life."

Truth: "God demonstrates his own love for us in this: While we were still sinners, Christ died for us" (Rom. 5:8).

Declaration: "God loves me more than I love myself. He knows me more than I know myself. He has my best interests in mind, and he can be trusted. If he 'did not spare his own Son, but gave him up for us all—how will he not also, along with him, graciously give us all things?'" (Rom. 8:32).

See how this life-transforming tool works? Remove the lie. Replace with truth.

I'll show you how this worked for me, using my confession of overworking.

For years I overachieved and overextended myself in unhealthy ways, just thinking of myself as a hard worker. Finally, I realized that what was driving me wasn't my work ethic but rather a desperate need to win the approval of other people. I wrongly believed my worth was based on what other people thought of me. I had to replace that lie with the truth.

The truth, not just for me but for you, is that our value is based not on what we do but on who made us (Ps. 139:13–16). That's why paintings that may look goofy to me are worth millions of dollars. Because if they were painted by Pablo Picasso, the value is in the hundreds of thousands or millions. So if God made me, I have tremendous value even if I do not have the approval of other people.

The truth, again not just for me but for you, is that our value is based not on how we feel about ourselves but on what someone else will pay for us (1 Peter 1:18–19). That's why a Lamborghini that might not impress you is actually worth three hundred thousand dollars. If someone is willing to pay that price, that's what it's worth. And if God

> **❝ THE TRUTH, NOT JUST FOR ME BUT FOR YOU, IS THAT OUR VALUE IS BASED NOT ON WHAT WE DO BUT ON WHO MADE US (PS. 139:13–16). ❞**

paid the price of his only son for me, I have infinite value regardless of what other people think of me.

So now whenever I think I need to impress people, I take that thought captive and make it obedient to Christ. The verb tense of "take captive" in the original language of the Bible implies a repeated and continuous action. This is not something you do once. This is something you will have to do thousands of times in your life, maybe dozens of times a day. The definition of a principle is a decision you make once and then live by.

Believe me, I am not saying this process is easy. I am still tempted to believe the lies, and I suspect you will be also. But these battles between our lies and God's truth are worth fighting! Because waging war as I have been training you to do in these pages is what will change your mind, redeem your thinking, and ultimately revolutionize your life.

— EXERCISE 3 —

DECLARING TRUTH

THIS EXERCISE BUILDS ON YOUR WORK IN EXERCISE 2.
Look back and use the lies you wrote there for this session. The
goal is to take what God is revealing to you and build helpful tools
to use in your life.

In this exercise, I want to give you the place and space to work
out your lies, truths, and declarations. In this chapter, we walked
through several examples in detail. Now it's time for you to work
through your own. For the truth in this book to truly change your
life, you will have to put in the personal work that I have had to
do over these past years and still do. The last thing you or I want
is for your life to look the same after you finish this book as it did
when you started.

Dig in, go deep, and allow God to show you his truth in his
Word. You will need to find truths in the Bible you can use as your
own, personal truths to replace the lies you are believing. A final
encouragement: anything you change in your life can affect future
generations and alter the course of your family line for Christ.

PART 1: THE REPLACEMENT PRINCIPLE

Lie:

Truth:

Declaration:

Lie:

Truth:

Declaration:

Lie:

Truth:

Declaration:

Lie:

Truth:

Declaration:

PART 2

THE REWIRE PRINCIPLE

Rewire Your Brain, Renew Your Mind

*Do not conform to the pattern of this world,
but be transformed by the renewing of
your mind. Then you will be able to test
and approve what God's will is—his good,
pleasing and perfect will.*

—ROMANS 12:2

CHAPTER 4

CROSSED WIRES AND CIRCULAR RUTS

MY FIRST CAR WAS NOT THE REGULAR 1979 BUICK CENTURY but the upgraded Buick Century, the model with a spoiler on the back. And spoiler alert: your grandpa's Buick did not have a spoiler!

What color, you ask? C'mon, what color car do you think someone with my unbridled coolness would have? Brown. Yeah, my car was an ugly brown. Yes, even the spoiler.

But wait! Did I mention the eagles? My Buick Century had an eagle sticker on each side, on the quarter panels just above the front tires! Those majestic eagles were descending from flight, talons out, ready to grab a tree branch and proclaim liberty for all. And I was ready to wow the ladies as I cruised into the school parking lot.

Only one problem. No, not my eighties shaggy, almost-a-mullet hairstyle and unibrow. The problem was the factory model stock stereo system Buick had installed in the car. I couldn't really fault them, though. Buick had no idea that I, someone as suave as Don Johnson on *Miami Vice*, with the dance moves of Patrick Swayze and the sheer animal magnetism of Maverick from *Top Gun*, would be driving their car in 1986. But I was. So I had to upgrade my ability to drive down the road with some thump-thump-thump rocking power.

I landed myself the coolest used Alpine stereo system I could find. *Yes!* Finally, I could blast some REO Speedwagon, some Van Halen, some one-arm-drummer Def Leppard. Now I could hear my favorite bands in full surround, supersonic, we-will-rock-you, make-my-ears-bleed, rock-your-face-off, I-can't-drive-fifty-five, we-built-this-city-on-rock-and-roll, quadraphonic super bass sound.

There was only one problem. Spending all my money buying the stereo system meant I couldn't afford to have it professionally installed. No, not a problem; I could install it! How hard could it be?

But I was and still am technically challenged. I can barely install a piece of bread into a toaster. Putting in my new car stereo in those pre–"watch a YouTube video to learn how to do anything" days was a nightmare. After working on the install all day, I still couldn't get the thing to work. Finally, by evening, with the eagles on my car soaring under the moon in the dark of night, I got my Alpine stereo to work! As the sun went down, the volume went up. Praise God from whom all blessings flow; he put the rock in my roll!

But the next morning, tragedy stuck. When I started my car and pushed the power button on my Alpine, I anticipated hearing a perfectly equalized version of the Police singing the stalker anthem "Every Breath You Take." But nothing happened. My self-installed, only-gently-used stereo didn't work. I pressed the button again. Pressed it harder. Nothing. *Why?!*

I could not get it to work all day long. Then, magically, that night it started working again. The next morning, dead. That night, mysteriously back to life again. Day after day, the same thing. During the day, nothing. Every night, perfect.

I figured out the pattern, but I could not find the problem. Some of you who are smarter than I was in 1986 have diagnosed the issue, haven't you?

Why would my car stereo work only at night?

Well, what electrical device do you tend to turn on at night in your car? Bingo!

I had crossed the wires.

Instead of wiring my car stereo to the proper source of power, I had wired it to my headlights. I could crank my tunes only with the lights on. So for the rest of the life of my 1979 Buick Century (with a spoiler; did I mention the spoiler?!), I was the dude driving around at two in the afternoon with my headlights on so I could listen to Bon Jovi. Sadly, I was not livin' on a prayer. I was livin' on the power of my headlights.

Why does it seem like our lives aren't working when we need them to work?

Why do we lack the power to live the way we want?

Why do we often make so many irrational and self-defeating decisions?

Why do we try so hard to change but end up doing the things we hate?

We have crossed wires.

You've seen it in yourself, right? I mean, why do you

- commit to stop arguing with your spouse, then keep arguing with your spouse?
- worry nonstop even though you know it's a waste of time and makes you sick?
- exaggerate to impress others even though that's not the kind of person you want to be?
- freak out because your credit card bill is so high, then continue to make more unnecessary purchases?
- scroll on your phone for hours instead of talking to your spouse and kids, who are sitting only a few feet away?
- decide you are going to lose weight and then find yourself grabbing a soda and candy bar when you stop to get gas?

You have crossed wires. We all do it.

The reason we make these poor decisions is because of how our brains work. So we need a solution that works with the way we think. We have to not only recognize the unhealthy patterns but also figure out the underlying problem. Stop the car, crawl under the dash, and find out what went wrong.

If we want to win the war in our minds, we have to be willing to rewire our thought patterns, rewire our brains.

STUCK IN A RUT

In Alaska there are only two seasons: winter and July. When the weather gets warm in the summer, the snow melts and the dirt roads become muddy. Cars drive on them, creating long ruts.

There is a sign along one Alaskan road that reads, "Choose your rut carefully. You'll be in it for the next sixty miles."

> **❝ IF WE WANT TO WIN THE WAR IN OUR MINDS, WE HAVE TO BE WILLING TO REWIRE OUR THOUGHT PATTERNS, REWIRE OUR BRAINS. ❞**

We all know what being in a rut feels like. Thinking the same thoughts, doing the same things, experiencing the same problems. It's like we're hopelessly entrenched on a muddy, rugged backroad.

And when a rut gets really deep, when your tires are all the way inside, you can let go of the steering wheel and the vehicle will just keep going down the road. Stuck in one direction with no options to get out or get off, until the rut ends.

So let's talk about how our brains work.

Every thought you have produces a neurochemical change in your mind. Your brain literally redesigns itself around that thought.

The brain is a command center that directs the parts of your body through neurons. Neurons link together to create messages. The same message sent multiple times will create a neural pathway. The presence of a neural pathway makes a thought easier to think and makes it easier for your body to send that same message again.

Think of neural pathways as ruts in your brain.

Now, how do ruts get created? Let me tell you about a cute little mini collie named Bandit that I once owned.

Oh, Bandit's color, you ask? C'mon, what color dog do you think someone with my unbridled coolness would have? Brown. Yes, my dog was the same color as my 1979 Buick Century (upgraded with the spoiler, eagle decals, and nighttime-only stereo—the car, not my dog.)

Bandit had a big yard to run around in but for some reason always ran in a circle in the exact same path. That pattern killed all the grass on his repeated, precise route and eventually created a circular rut that made it look like an alien spaceship had landed in our yard.

In a similar way, repeated thoughts create paths in our brains. Again, neural pathways are brain ruts.

These ruts are often carved deeper by the bundle of nerves at the base of our brain stem known as the reticular activating system (RAS). The RAS sifts through millions of pieces of sensory data being sent to our brains and groups them according to relevance and similarity. If the information will keep us alive, prevent problems, avert danger, or bring pleasure, the RAS is activated. It's your brain's system for filtering through all the data in your life and allowing you to focus on what's most pertinent and ignore the rest.

Our RASs also utilize our established beliefs to screen incoming information. This is part of the reason we so often get what we expect. If you keep thinking you're a victim who never has a steady job or long-lasting relationships, you are training your brain to look for evidence which supports that belief and to filter out evidence which doesn't. You condition your brain to reinforce what you already believe. You create a victim rut. The tires drop in, you let go of the steering wheel, and you travel down the victim road.

Your brain is designed to look for patterns and create neurological pathways to help you keep thinking the things you keep thinking and doing the things you keep doing.

This is why thinking new thoughts or trying new things is awkward the first time. Remember when you first tried to ride a bike or play the piano or do calculus? You thought it would never happen. But as you think that thought or do that thing again and again, it becomes effortless. (Except for maybe calculus. But you know what I mean.) The saying "Practice makes perfect" makes even more sense now, doesn't it?

Thinking that thought or doing that thing again and again eventually becomes effortless. Remember how great you got at explaining your favorite hobby or playing a sport or game? The more often you did it, the easier it became. Unknowingly, you created these well-traveled neural pathways that made something easier that was once difficult.

Years ago my wife, Amy, and I wanted to learn some basic ballroom dancing skills. We didn't want to pay for real lessons, so we rented a video. One dance move was how to get out of a corner. At first we kept bumping into each other. After we bumbled through it a few dozen times, it started to get easier and our feet began to flow together. Invite us to a dance today, and you will see that we are get-out-of-the-corner experts.

The more you do something, the more natural it becomes. Of course, you already knew that, but you may never have understood why. As a neural pathway forms in your brain, thinking a thought or taking an action can go from very difficult to very easy. With enough repetition, falling into a neurological rut will become automatic.

God created neural pathways to be a good thing. When you learned to drive, you were unsure of yourself; you fumbled through it, going too easy on the gas and slamming on the brakes, turning the wrong way when you drove in reverse. Today driving is simple for you.

Have you ever been driving on a long road trip, gone deep into thought, and then after several minutes went by, suddenly snapped out of it? Who was driving while you were momentarily checked out? Well, you were. How? By means of your developed neural pathways.

Repetition formed helpful ruts.

But because of our sin, neural pathways can also be a bad thing. Why? The same reason you felt awkward the first time you

- tried to eat away your depressed feelings with a Snickers.
- thought of yourself as a victim who can never win.
- responded to a bad experience by going shopping and spending way too much money.
- passed along some juicy but hurtful gossip about a good friend.

Feeling uncomfortable, you thought, *This is dumb. Why am I doing this?* You may have felt guilty. But you also got a little jolt of pleasure. That buzz is a chemical your brain releases called dopamine. That little natural high is your brain's way of saying, *I like that. Let's think that again! Let's do that again!*

So you checked out the cute trainer at the gym again, drank another glass of wine when you were stressed, or lied to a friend to get out of something. This time felt a little less awkward, and you got another hit of dopamine. That led you to do it again. The third time was much easier. Why? You were developing a neural pathway. Do the same thing enough, and you will have a rut that you fall into automatically.

You were designed to smoothly, efficiently create and fall into habits, into neurological ruts.

That is helpful for brushing your teeth.

That is harmful for overeating.

If you find yourself stuck in unhealthy ruts, there's some good news: God has given us a way out. And you don't have to wait until you're driving in Alaska in July.

RECOGNIZING THE RUT

In part 1, we worked on identifying the lies we believe. We agreed that lies can be hard to detect, so it helps to identify the problems that plague us.

As you think about what you think about, you might notice some common harmful thought patterns. I know I do. We are wise to recognize these mental ruts we repeatedly travel that divert us from the path we know God wants us to be on.

One of my most frustrating mental ruts involves finances. I am always tempted to believe the lie that I can find security in money instead of in God. Hey, just being real. But in my heart I know and believe that God is my provider. Yet my thoughts get trapped in the same old rut of worrying that I won't have enough to provide security and stability for the people I love.

So I identified a lie I believe that leads me into an irrational, self-defeating mental rut. What should I do next? You know from the previous chapter: ask probing questions.

Why do I believe this lie? When did this false belief start?

My grandmother (who is in heaven now) is one of my heroes. I respected her so much, and her words meant everything to me. Grandma and I used to love to sit on her front porch and watch the cars pass in front of her house.

She loved to tell me stories about the funny things my mom did when she was a little girl. Grandma would smoke her cigarettes as she told me the same stories again and again. I would eat a cherry-flavored popsicle and laugh like I was hearing them all for the very first time. The conversation was always light and playful. Until one day when it wasn't.

I'm not sure why she chose that particular day to tell me about her childhood during the Great Depression. Although I did not fully understand her thinking back then, I clearly understand the effect it has had on my thinking to this day.

I sat on Grandma's lap as she shifted from storyteller to teacher. She did her best to explain to me what sparked the Great Depression. Then she started shaking as she recalled the horrors that she, like so many others in her generation, had suffered through. She cried as she described people eating out of garbage cans to survive and those who had lost hope and jumped out of windows. Grandma looked me in the eyes and warned, "Craig, I love you so much. You need to know that the economy *will* fall apart again in your lifetime. And when it does, you need to be ready."

That idea was new and confusing, but I believed my grandma. I started worrying about money, dreading the day when I wouldn't have enough. So if someone gave me cash for my birthday, I would hide it under my rug. The slow-growing little lump in my bedroom floor represented where I was putting my hope. Someday the economy would crash, but I would be able to buy food for my family. I was doing exactly what Grandma had warned me to do.

You might think that as I got older, I would rationally assess the economic climate of the world and my personal financial situation. Nope. My brain had already formed neural pathways. So every time I thought about money, my reflex reaction was to worry and try to create financial security.

I worked hard to pay off any and every debt. Just five years into our marriage, Amy and I had paid off all of our debt, including the mortgage on our small house. Being debt free puts you in a strong financial position that should lead to freedom. Not for me. Money and security were still a constant source of anxiety. I still made irrational decisions. Even ordering what I wanted at a restaurant was difficult for me. If cheese cost extra, I wouldn't add it to my burger. Pretty stupid, right? Could I afford the extra fifty cents? Of course, but it was almost impossible for me to think that way.

My mindset was driven by a deep fear of scarcity and poverty, even while owing no one and making enough money. Why? I had spent years developing neural pathways, and the easiest thing was for me to fall into those same unhealthy mental ruts.

What about you? What's your rut?

Maybe when you were young, your mom's answer for every problem was food. When you were a baby, she gave you a bottle when you cried. When you were a toddler, if you fell down and skinned your knee, the solution wasn't a bandaid but ice cream. During your high school years, when you were devastated by a breakup, she made brownies.

What happened to you?

Your brain created a neural pathway. Neurons linked together, over and over, with the same message: if you are hurt or angry or sad, eat something; comfort yourself with food. Now eating is your built-in response to a problem.

Perhaps on the first day of first grade, you were picked last on the playground for kickball. You tried to make sense of that strange new feeling. What did it mean?

Then your father didn't treat you fairly, which felt familiar, a lot like what happened at recess.

All through middle school, your sibling was more popular than you, so you thought, perhaps subconsciously, *Huh, this is kind of like what happened on the playground and with Dad.*

Then your parents told you they were getting a divorce. *What? No! Why is this happening to me? My friends' parents aren't divorced. Bad things like this are always happening to me! It's like I'm cursed.*

What happened to you?

Your brain created a neural pathway. You began weaving these random, different, yet somehow similar experiences into a story you told yourself. You started to believe a lie that you are a victim. You can't win. People will always hurt you. Now, almost no matter what happens, your habitual response is to think that someone's out to get you and something is about to go wrong.

Maybe you went off to college and felt very lonely there. You had no friends yet and felt like you didn't fit in. What you did have was your parents' credit card. So you drove to the mall and bought some new clothes. Having something new and nice, imagining how you'd look in it, led your brain to release some dopamine. That natural high was the first time you had felt good in weeks. Your brain responded, *That felt good. Do that again!*

You did. A few weeks later you received a bad grade. You went to the mall and bought something. Then you went through a painful breakup. You went to the mall and bought something.

What happened to you?

Your brain created a neural pathway. You've been doing the same thing for so long, it's like you made one of my dog Bandit's crop circles, except the rut you created runs back and forth from your house to the mall. When you are disappointed, when you feel like you are not enough, when you are angry, you buy something you cannot afford. And now it's all on the credit card, which compounds the problem.

One night when you were a teenager, you finished your homework and got bored. You started mindlessly surfing the internet, and then it happened. One click at a time, you wandered onto a site that showed seductive photos of a barely clothed body.

You felt awkward and guilty but also excited. You hit a dopamine jackpot.

The next time you were bored, the thought hit you: *I could try to find that website.* You did, and it was a little less awkward with a little less guilt.

A couple of days later you were bored again, and you quickly decided to find that same website. Actually, why not see what else is out there? You found new sites with nudity, and this time it all felt more intuitive.

Pretty soon you were making excuses to get alone in your bedroom, because all day you were thinking about finding more websites and seeing more stimulating images and videos.

What happened to you?

Your brain created a neural pathway. God's original intention for you to have a pure mind was violated, and you began thinking thoughts you were never intended to think.

A WAKE-UP CALL

In all these examples, including my own, wires got crossed. Normal life events occurred, fair or not, intentional or not, and we turned the opportunity into a bad connection that formed an unhealthy pattern that created a toxic rut. In the case of my grandma's advice, I could still have made the healthy decision to be frugal and live debt free but also taken her stories as prompts to be generous to the down-and-out and be grateful for all my blessings.

And Bandit? Well, he stayed on that same path with that same pattern for all of his dog years.

Unless we decide to break the pattern, our lives will continue moving in the wrong direction. In a circle that never goes anywhere. It's normal. Easy. The same old rut.

I'm guessing you want something different, something better. Maybe that's the only reason you picked up this book.

I finally recognized the unintended consequences of my financial rut and realized that I had to change. It happened one night at a restaurant called Applewoods. I am crazy about my kids and

> **UNLESS WE DECIDE TO BREAK THE PATTERN, OUR LIVES WILL CONTINUE MOVING IN THE WRONG DIRECTION.**

have established a special birthday celebration with my daughters. The birthday girl gets all dolled up. Daddy drives to the house and picks her up, carrying a small bouquet of her favorite flowers. Daddy asks, "What restaurant do you want to go to?" and acts surprised when she picks Applewoods. They always pick Applewoods. Why? Because they give free, all-you-can-eat apple fritters. God is good all the time, and all the time God is good.

The birthday of my oldest daughter, Catie, arrived, and she looked even more beautiful than she usually does, with her hair curled for the big night. Once we were seated at the restaurant, I said, "Sweetheart, happy birthday. Order whatever you want. Go for it."

As she was looking at the menu, the waitress walked up, so I asked, "Catie, are you ready to order?" She answered, "Daddy, I can't." The waitress was now standing at our table, smiling and waiting. I told Catie, "Princess, order whatever you want. It's your birthday."

Her eyes started to tear up. "Daddy, I can't. What I want costs too much money."

Her words shook me to my core. We weren't at a five-star restaurant, or even a four-star. We were at Applewoods! The Google description has only two dollar signs.

I realized I had unintentionally taught her to think about money like I did. Just as my grandmother unintentionally passed on her fears to me. My own unhealthy mindset had revealed itself in my precious daughter. I did not want her to live in fear as I did. At that moment I vowed I would end this. I would not pass down this ongoing personal problem to someone I love. I had to attack this city and demolish this. Which meant I would need God's power in a major way.

Since age seven, I'd been stuck in irrational, self-defeating thinking about finances. For decades I believed the lies: *I won't have enough. My family will suffer. We can't afford to spend money. We need to plan for the bad times that are just around the corner.*

But that night with Catie was a wake-up call from God. He got my attention with her words. The truth was that we did have enough, yet my family was still suffering. Not from a lack of money but from my mindset being passed to my kids. I thought we couldn't afford some material things, but the reality was I could no longer afford to stay in my rut, driven by fear. My family didn't need anything except for me to make a paradigm shift in how I viewed God's obvious provision and blessings.

My brain had thought the same thoughts for so long, and I needed a solution that worked with the way my brain works.

I had a rut. But what I needed God to do then was to give me a new rut.

—— EXERCISE 4 ——

RECOGNIZING YOUR RUTS

IN THIS EXERCISE, I WANT YOU TO WRITE DOWN ANY PLACES in your life where lies have crossed your wires and created ruts in your thinking. Using what you wrote in exercise 3 and considering the many examples I gave you in this chapter, ask God to speak to you and reveal the origin of your ruts. If at all possible, as in the situation with my grandma, try to go back to the source.

Whether or not you can discover where these things began, the primary goal of this exercise is to write down and face any and every harmful, hurtful rut that has been created in your mind. You are walking through a personal journey, one step at a time, that can lead you to a renewed mind and a changed life.

My ruts:

Crossed Wires and Circular Ruts

CHAPTER 5

CREATING A TRENCH
OF TRUTH

A WHILE BACK I MADE A SOLEMN VOW THAT I WOULD STOP obsessing over texts and emails. I decided that anytime I heard the bing indicating I had received a message, I would not feel the urgency to check immediately. And when I did check, I would not reread and reread what the other person wrote. I would then not rewrite and rewrite my response. My digital resolution lasted . . . well, honestly, I don't think I ever stopped obsessing over texts and emails. Not only did my vow not last; I didn't even start!

The problem with how we attack our problems is that we go after the problem. We focus solely on the behavior by making a commitment to start or stop doing something.

You've done this too, right? You've decided, perhaps even declared, that you were going to change.

- I'm going to quit smoking on January 1st!
- This year I'm going to eat healthy and exercise every day!
- I'm going to stop dating anyone who is mean to me. In fact, I'm not going to date at all!
- I'm tired of wasting my time on social media and comparing my life with everyone else's. I'm getting off for good this time!
- That's it. This is the last time. I will never look at pornography again!
- I'm not going to exaggerate or lie or gossip to get attention or feel better about myself. No more!
- I'm going to read the Bible every morning this whole year!

Whatever your vow was, how did it go?

I would guess not well. Why? Behavior modification doesn't work, because the focus is only on modifying behavior. You don't get to the root of the problem, which is the thought that produces the behavior. To be more specific, the problem is the neural pathway that leads to the behavior.

Let's say you hate an ugly tree in your yard. You want that tree gone. Finally, you decide the time has come to take care of the problem. So you march into your yard with a small handsaw. You pick an ugly branch and cut it off the tree. You smile and walk back into the house, triumphantly singing a medley of "All I Do Is Win" and "Another One Bites the Dust." The next day you are shocked to see that the tree is still standing strong. As you stare out the window, you could almost swear it's smirking at you.

I know. The analogy is absurd. You would never try to kill a tree by just removing a branch. Because the branch obviously isn't the problem. The tree is the problem. Actually, the root system of the tree is the main culprit. If you don't remove the root system when you cut down the tree, it could still grow back.

Here's a different spin: You start coughing a lot. You go to the doctor. He tells you that you have lung cancer. You decide to start popping cough drops to stop your cough. Of course, you would never do that. You would realize that the cough is just a symptom of the real problem. What you need to attack is the cancer, not the cough.

Well, if we decide, *I'm going to stop yelling at my kids* or *I'm going to stop isolating myself and living a lonely life* or *I'm going to exercise every day*, we're just sawing off a branch or taking a cough drop. We are ignoring the real problem of the lie we believe and the mental rut we fall into. Attacking only symptoms, not the source.

Thinking I can change a behavior just by removing the behavior is absurd. The behavior isn't the root problem. The neural pathway that leads me to the behavior is the problem. If I stop a behavior, it will come back, unless I

1. remove the lie at the root of the behavior, and
2. replace the neural pathway that leads me to the behavior.

Throughout part 1, we learned how to remove the lie and replace it with truth. Now let's discover how we can create a new neural pathway, or to put it another way, dig a new and helpful trench. This is going to help us rewire our brains and renew our minds.

To make sure we understand what we're talking about, let's spell out the differences between our two similar words:

A *rut* is typically formed in mud and becomes a nuisance, even a danger. A rut is unintentionally created, has no purpose, and requires repair.

A *trench* is intentionally dug to deliver a necessary resource. A trench has a specific purpose and fixes an existing problem.

We know that the only antidote for a lie is truth. That's why our first tool was the Replacement Principle: Remove the lies, replace with truth. The antidote for a negative neural pathway is a new neural pathway. Instead of living in a rut, you can create a truth trench that runs deeper, diverting the flow of your thoughts from old pathways to new ones.

We have a series of set thoughts we think each time we are triggered. For you, the trigger might be feeling alone, fearing failure, or being around people who are drinking; you fall into the same series of thoughts you always fall into, and they lead to the same behavior. We are now going to strategically choose a new series of thoughts.

Where will we get these new thoughts? Hint: we won't get them from scrolling through social media posts, listening to our favorite playlist, or phoning a friend for their opinion.

To stop the lies and replace them with truth, we need to look to God's Word.

Remember, that's the weapon God gives us for the battle we are fighting. His truth is what can set us free, and we are going to choose specific Bible verses to create a new neural pathway that applies directly to our problem. Using his Word, we will create a trench of truth.

> **TO STOP THE LIES AND REPLACE THEM WITH TRUTH, WE NEED TO LOOK TO GOD'S WORD.**

For this to work, we need to do more than just know God's Word; we need to internalize it. The author of Psalm 119 understood this when he wrote, "I have hidden your word in my heart that I might not sin against you" (v. 11).

That's what Jesus did. He had verses memorized that applied directly to temptations he faced. When Satan tempted him, Jesus couldn't whip out his iPhone and open up the YouVersion Bible app to search for a verse that might help. He had already internalized truths from God's Word that created a helpful neural pathway. When tempted, Jesus followed that path, leading him to obedience and freedom.

That's what we need to do.

So let's see how another tool can empower us to overcome the unhelpful and unhealthy patterns that have held us hostage and kept us from the life God intends for us to live.

DETERMINING DECLARATIONS

The second tool for changing your thinking is the Rewire Principle: Rewire your brain, renew your mind. I told you earlier about my financial rut. Any trigger about money leads me to fear, thoughts of how I don't have enough, and my need to save more to create security. When I am triggered about money, I fall into a rut—that's the way my brain works—so I need to create a trench of truth.

The good news is that the Bible speaks to all our problems. God's Word gives us truth that empowers us to break out of the old ruts of destruction and onto a new path that leads to life. What does the Bible say that applies directly to my fears and issues about money? Here are some of my verses:

- "I know what it is to be in need, and I know what it is to have plenty. I have learned the secret of being content in any and every situation, whether well fed or hungry, whether living in plenty or in want" (Phil. 4:12).
- "I will save you, and you will be a blessing" (Zech. 8:13).
- "It is more blessed to give than to receive" (Acts 20:35).
- "God is able to bless you abundantly, so that in all things at all times, having all that you need, you will abound in every good work" (2 Cor. 9:8).
- "God will meet all your needs according to the riches of his glory in Christ Jesus" (Phil. 4:19).

From these I put together what I call a "declaration"—what I am declaring to be true in my battle against the lies I am tempted to believe. The goal of the declaration is to have it become my new neural pathway, my intentionally dug trench of truth.

Here's my declaration based on God's Word:

Money is not and never will be a problem for me.
My God is an abundant provider who meets every
need.
Because I am blessed, I will always be a blessing.
I will lead the way with irrational generosity, because
I know it's truly more blessed to give than to
receive.

That's just one of my declarations that speaks directly to a problem that has plagued me for years. These statements create a new pathway, leading me to a life of peace and generosity.

What new neural pathway do you need to create? That depends on your old pathway, right?

Let's go back to some of our past examples. In your old rut the paradigm was, if you are hurt or angry or sad, eat something. You look up Bible verses about food and eating and what to do when you are struggling. You find:

- "You must honor God with your body" (1 Cor. 6:20 NLT).
- "Jesus replied, 'I am the bread of life. Whoever comes to me will never be hungry again'" (John 6:35 NLT).
- "LORD, my strength and my fortress, my refuge in time of distress" (Jer. 16:19).

Inspired by the truth of God's Word, you write your declaration:

When I am stressed or in times of distress, I turn
to God, not food.
I come to Jesus because he is what I really need.
He is my strength, my fortress, and my refuge.

Now every time you are hurt or angry or sad, you prayerfully and with Jesus-inspired confidence proclaim your declaration.

In your old rut, you saw yourself as a victim who could never win. You've wrongly believed that people are out to get you, will hurt you, and will let you down. That has not led you into the life you want, so you create a trench of truth using verses you find in Romans 8. Your declaration could be:

God is for me, so who can be against me?
My God is working all things for my good.
I am more than a conqueror through Jesus, who
loves me and gives me strength.

Your old rut led you to buy things you couldn't afford, rationalizing that you deserve it and shouldn't be deprived of nice things. Now you create a new trench of truth with God's Word:

I am not my stuff. I am who God says I am.
He says I am blessed, fulfilled, and called to make a
difference.

> My God has given me everything I need for life and
>   godliness.
> I am content and full of joy because he is enough.

Maybe you have struggled with lust for years. When you're online, at the gym, or anywhere, your eyes and thoughts go places you know they shouldn't. So you create a declaration, based on truths found in God's Word, that becomes your new neural pathway, your trench of truth:

> Lust is not my master.
> God has redeemed me and given me pure thoughts.
> I will not look lustfully, because I've made that
>   covenant with my eyes and with my God, who
>   strengthens me.
> God is always faithful and, when I am tempted, will
>   always provide a way out.

Draw your declarations from God's truth and make them your own. Be creative. Write your declarations in a way that will speak to and inspire you. Put them in places where you can quickly see them and memorize them. Put them in the notes on your phone so you can immediately swipe away and scroll to them. Record them in your voice memos and listen as you exercise or drive. Repetition will dig your new trench deeper and deeper, making the new pathway easier and more accessible.

Write your declaration as if it were already true, even if you don't fully believe it yet. With a new declaration, we are claiming the victory we have in Christ, and we need to create a neural pathway that affirms our ability to demolish the stronghold and win the battle.

All this might feel foolish at first. Remember, anything new can feel strange in the beginning. You will be saying something you want to believe, but your life will be saying something different. That's okay. Don't be discouraged. Don't give up. The gravitational pull toward your old negative thoughts will likely be stronger than you can imagine. Resist those lies. Keep renewing your mind with God's truth, and it will become true of you.

WRITE IT, THINK IT, CONFESS IT

For years I thought that if I went to the gym, threw some weights around, and grunted a lot, I would somehow be in good physical shape. What I didn't realize was that even more than what I do *with* my body, physical fitness is about what I put *in* my body. If I am to be truly healthy, what goes into me has to be healthy.

The same is true with our minds. What we put in our minds comes out in our lives. Every action we take, every word we say, and every attitude we express originates in our thoughts.

But what's crazy is how little attention we give to what goes into our minds. People who have high-performance cars put in only high-octane gasoline. People who care about their dogs choose pet food that has antioxidants and the right balance of meats, vegetables, grains, and fruits. We can be so careful about what we put into our cars or feed our pets yet so careless about what we put into our minds.

One reason we need to be extra attentive about these decisions is because we constantly have thoughts that we did not choose. Studies reveal that we are bombarded by about five hundred unintentional and intrusive thoughts a day.[2] Each unwanted thought lasts about fourteen seconds. Do the math. That's almost two hours a day of thoughts we do not want to think.

Two hours of thought missiles like, *You aren't good enough. You deserve better. You will always struggle with your weight. If they knew you, they wouldn't like you. You will always be alone.* If we don't do something, those thoughts will poison our thinking. We really do need to win the war in our minds!

Psychologists and others who study how our minds work talk about the law of exposure. The law of exposure says that the mind absorbs and reflects what it is exposed to the most. Basically, if we allow a thought into our minds, it will come out in our lives.

More than two thousand years ago, our thoughtology professor Paul taught us that same truth when he wrote, "Those who are dominated by the sinful nature think about sinful things, but those who are controlled by the Holy Spirit think about things that please the Spirit. So letting your sinful nature control your mind leads to death. But letting the Spirit control your mind leads to life and peace" (Rom. 8:5–6 NLT).

Paul taught that if you allow a thought into your mind, it will come out in your life. So if you want to change your life, you have to change your thinking. You need a new declaration.

We need to be diligent about what we allow into our minds! Why? Because what consumes our minds controls our lives.

> **IF YOU WANT TO CHANGE YOUR LIFE, YOU HAVE TO CHANGE YOUR THINKING.**

That's why I meditate on truth, specifically on Bible verses that apply to my strongholds and on the declarations I have written to create new neural pathways.

Now, I don't know what springs to mind for you when you encounter the word meditation, but I can tell you what the biblical understanding of it is: focusing one's thoughts on the things of God. The Bible talks *a lot* about meditating. We are told to focus on, to meditate on, God's goodness and God's Word.

Eastern meditation is an emptying of your mind. What I'm suggesting—what the Bible calls for—is the opposite. Christian meditation is filling your mind with God's truth, being strategic and deliberate about what you allow into your mind. We make the law of exposure work for us instead of against us. We win the war in our minds by creating a solution for our mental ruts: trenches of truth that work with the way our brains work.

We'll talk more about meditation in the next chapter, but for now I want to encourage you to meditate on the truths that apply to your problem. Here's the plan: write it, think it, and confess it until you believe it.

I shared earlier that I have struggled since childhood with negative thinking about myself. I have felt like I'm not good enough and need to prove myself. I often feel overwhelmed, like I will never get it all done.

My negative thoughts created unhealthy neural pathways. Finally, I decided that I would not stay stuck in those ruts but would instead create positive, God-honoring pathways in my mind. To expose the lie and embrace truth, I needed to create a new trench of truth. So I wrote the following faith declarations to replace the lies in my mind with God's truth.

Jesus is first in my life.
I exist to serve and glorify him.

I love my wife, and I will lay down my life to serve her.

I will raise my children to love God and serve him
   with their whole hearts.
I will nurture, equip, train, and empower them to do
   more for the kingdom than they ever thought
   possible.

I love people. And believe the best about others.

I am disciplined.
Christ in me is stronger than the wrong desires in me.

I am growing closer to Jesus every day.
Because of Christ, my family is closer, my body is
    stronger, my faith is deeper, my leadership is
    sharper.

I am creative, innovative, driven, focused, and
    blessed beyond measure because the Spirit of
    God dwells within me.

Money is not and never will be a problem for me.
My God is an abundant provider who meets every
    need.
Because I am blessed, I will always be a blessing.
I will lead the way with irrational generosity, because
    I know it's truly more blessed to give than to
    receive.

I develop leaders. That's not something I do; it's
    who I am.

Pain is my friend. I rejoice in suffering, because
    Jesus suffered for me.

I bring my best and then some.
It's what I bring after I bring my best that makes the difference.

The world will be different and better because I served Jesus today.

What do I do with these declarations? I meditate on them by writing, thinking, and confessing these truths until I believe them. When I repeat these declarations again and again, scientifically speaking I am creating new neural pathways. I am digging trenches of truth deeper and deeper for the purpose of changing my mind and my life. And, as I shared about my daughter Catie at the restaurant, I will change my family legacy.

I am allowing God's truth to renew my mind.

That's our plan:

- Identify the rut.
- Create a new trench of truth with God's truth.
- Write a declaration, think it, and confess it until you believe it.

This will take some work. It will not be easy. But if you will put in the time and energy, you will create new trenches of truth so God can renew your mind.

And when you change your thinking, you will change your life.

—— EXERCISE 5 ——

DIGGING TRENCHES OF TRUTH

IN THIS CHAPTER, WE DUG EVEN DEEPER INTO WHAT IT means to meditate on God's Word and then convert biblical principles into lifelong declarations. I want to give you another opportunity to pray and ask God for trenches of truth and declarations to remove the lies you've been believing. I've shown you my declarations, which I've used for years and will continue to use; now focus on your own. Dig your trenches of truth deep, allowing God to renew your mind and transform your life. Remember:

Write it. Think it. Confess it. Until you believe it.

Lie:

Truth:

Declaration:

Lie:

Truth:

Declaration:

CHAPTER 6

RUMINATION AND RENEWAL

I APOLOGIZE IN ADVANCE, BUT I AM ABOUT TO GROSS YOU out. But, well, it's necessary and for your own good.

In Joshua 1:8, Psalm 1:2, and at least six other passages in the Psalms, God tells us to ruminate. The word meditate in these verses is the same as the word ruminate. What does ruminate mean? Rumination is what cows do with their cud. (Sorry, this is where things get weird.)

Cows get a mouthful of grass, chew it up, swallow it, throw it back up in their mouths, chew it some more, swallow it again, throw it back up into their mouths again, chew it some more, swallow it again, throw it back up again, chew it more, swallow it again. They do this over and over and over. That is what it means to ruminate.

That is the exact idea behind the word meditate. Meditating is taking a thought—in our case a Bible verse or a declaration based on God's Word—and chewing on it, then swallowing it, then bringing it back to mind and chewing on it some more. Then we swallow it again, then bring it back to mind and chew on it more. We do that over and over and over. We aren't talking about casual Bible reading; we mean repeatedly taking in every word, the meaning, and the context.

Why? Well, why do cows ruminate on their cud? Because it allows them to get the maximum amount of nutrition out of the grass.

Why do we meditate on God's truth and God's love and God's great deeds? One reason is because it allows us to get the maximum amount of spiritual nutrition out of our godly thoughts.

There's another reason: repetition is the reason for ruts.

When you envision my dog Bandit running around the yard, or people driving on a muddy road in Alaska, it's obvious that one time does not a rut make. The reason for a physical rut is repetition.

The same is true for our mental ruts. Want to hear something fascinating? Increasingly research proves that the way to get someone to believe a lie is to simply repeat the lie.[3] Psychologists call this the illusory truth effect. It's been called a glitch in the human psyche.

The reason we're so likely to believe something we hear repeatedly is because we use only 10 percent of our brains. Our inability to engage more of our brain capacity hinders us from distinguishing truth from mistruth.

Except, guess what? We *don't* use only 10 percent of our brains! That's a lie. But a lie most people believe. Why? Because it has been stated repeatedly. Just like vitamin C can help prevent or cure the common cold. It can't. People just say it can. And because people have said it enough, people believe it.

Repetition is the reason for ruts.

This is why our spiritual enemy has been whispering the same lies to us repeatedly our entire lives. He knows that the more often we think a thought, the more likely we are to believe it, and the more likely it is for the lie to become a rut we get stuck in.

> **❝ OUR SPIRITUAL ENEMY HAS BEEN WHISPERING THE SAME LIES TO US REPEATEDLY OUR ENTIRE LIVES. ❞**

Have you noticed that the devil keeps whispering the same lies to you? He is just being repetitive, not creative. If he were creative, today he'd tempt you to fight with your spouse, and tomorrow with your mail carrier. But my guess is that it's always your spouse, and you might not even know who delivers your mail. If Satan were creative, today he'd tell you you're not pretty enough, and tomorrow that you don't perspire enough. But I bet you've never feared that you lack the ability to sweat.

Satan is not very creative. He is very repetitive. He knows that if he tells you a lie often enough, you will eventually believe it.

So how will you overcome his lies? How will you replace the old rut with a new pathway? The answer is repetition.

You are going to write it, think it, and confess it until you believe it.

Speaking your declarations once will not really do anything. You have been told lies over and over, and you now need to tell yourself the truth over and over. Meditate, chew, ruminate, swallow, repeat. As Napoleon Hill said, "Any idea, plan, or purpose may be placed in the mind by repetition of thought." Repetition is what created the old rut. Repetition is what will create the new trench.

Write it, think it, confess it until you believe it.

Do this as early as possible each morning. What we are thinking about now influences what we think about next. So what you think about first thing in the morning is the first domino to fall, impacting your thoughts for the rest of the day.

What does that mean?

You should start your day in God's Word, digging trenches of truth and finding your declarations. Then write it, think it, confess it until you believe it.

PARLEZ-VOUS GROESCHEL

Linguistic experts tell us that a new word is invented every ninety-eight minutes.[4] That may make it seem like we're getting a lot of new words, but there are still necessary words that haven't been invented yet, except by me:

- People today often work from a "mobile office." When you call and ask where they are, they answer, "Well, I'm . . . well, at my office . . . but my office is at a coffee shop." (Two lattes a day is cheaper than rent.) Enough equivocating. Let's just invent a word: *moffice*. Pronounced "ma-fis." Moffice is your mobile office.

- You probably have a friend who is always looking at their Apple Watch. Let's call those people *watch-watchers*. See that? I just invented another word in less than ninety-eight minutes.
- Here's a new verb: *alexing*. Alexing is getting information from Alexa. When you ask, "Alexa, how's the weather?" you are alexing.

We may need some new words, but the word I want you to understand now is an actual word: *automaticity*. Automaticity is the ability to do things without thinking about what you are doing. When repetition allows an action to become unconscious, automatic.

When you take a shower, you don't wonder, *What part of me should I wash first? How do I wash my hair? There are so many things to think about.* No, you get in the shower and do everything you need to do without thinking. While one part of your brain is taking care of cleaning you up, another part is thinking about the day to come or the day you just had. Automaticity.

But automaticity is also why you keep doing things you don't want to do. Repetition has led to negative, harmful things becoming automatic.

The goal of meditating on God's Word and on our declarations is automaticity. We want to fall into the new trench, which will lead us into the right thoughts and actions. Automatically. An old quote states, "Watch your thoughts, they become your words; watch your words, they become your actions; watch your actions, they become your habits; watch your habits, they become your character; watch your character, it becomes your destiny." The journey to your destiny starts with your thoughts. The right thoughts lead to the right life. Automatically.

Zig Ziglar said, "Repetition is the mother of learning and the father of action, which makes it the architect of accomplishment."

> 66 THE JOURNEY TO YOUR DESTINY STARTS WITH YOUR THOUGHTS. THE RIGHT THOUGHTS LEAD TO THE RIGHT LIFE. 99

I studied French from eighth grade all the way through high school. I sat through class and took all the tests, but I never actually tried to speak French.

When I was in eleventh grade, a foreign exchange student from France moved to our school. She was cute! I knew that if she could just see me in the parking lot, she'd be dazzled by my dirt-brown Buick. I could flip on the headlights, crank some Huey Lewis—"that's the p-p-power of love"—and watch her heart get snatched up by the talons of my majestic above-the-tire eagles.

Unfortunately, we were never in the parking lot at the same time. No problem. I could impress her with my ability to *parlez-vous français*. After all, I was in my fourth year of her native tongue.

I walked over to her one day and tried to talk to her in French. IT WAS SO BAD.

I quickly discovered I could not speak French and found myself doing a bad Pepé Le Pew impersonation, saying with a pathetic French accent, "Oh, mon chéri. The devotion. The longing. How about you stop resisting me and I'll stop resisting you?" (If you're under, say, thirtyish, just search for "Pepé Le Pew" on YouTube for your animated enlightenment.)

When I realized that I was speaking not in French but in English with a cheesy quasi-French accent, I panicked. I thought, *Say something in French, Groeschel!* Suddenly I found myself talking about French fries and waxing eloquent about French onion soup. *No, Groeschel. You are dying here! Do something!*

That's when she started speaking French to me. I listened and thought, *Oh no, this is all in French. I've got to translate this into English in my mind!* I heard her words and quickly tried to think of the English equivalents. Then I thought in English of how I wanted to reply. Then I translated it in my brain. Then, finally, I tried to speak to her in French. "So, mon chéri. Could I make you some . . . French toast?" Train wreck.

Day after day we had these cringeworthy, awkward, embarrassing conversations, until finally something clicked. She spoke in French, I understood her in French, and then I responded in French! Somehow, suddenly, the wires crossed (or uncrossed?) in my brain, and I had a fluency (automaticity) in French.

That's our goal. (No, not to speak French.) With God's help, we are going to uncross the wires. Instead of living by lies, we will embrace God's truth. Chances are you might even know what's true. But knowing it doesn't mean you believe it.

Don't give up. Keep moving forward. Write it, think it, confess it until you believe it. You are rewiring your brain. God is renewing your mind. Then one day something will click. You will be fluent in truth. Automaticity. You will have changed your thinking, and it will change your life.

That's what happened to me.

DECLARING VICTORY

As someone who struggled with fear about money and finances, I always experienced tax season as a time of great stress. Would we get a refund? *Dear Jesus, let us get a refund!* Or would we owe money? *Dear Jesus, please don't let us owe money!* One year our CPA told us a few weeks early that we were in good shape and likely to get a small refund. *Yes!* A week later he realized he'd made a significant mistake. We actually were going to owe several thousand dollars. *Nooooo!*

It wasn't the end of the world. We had enough money in savings to cut a check. It really didn't impact our lives that much, but it did send me into a mental spiral. I couldn't eat. I couldn't sleep. I couldn't talk about the issue with my family.

At two in the morning, I was lying in bed, wide awake. I was scared, but something else was happening. For the first time in my life, I felt myself being pulled in the other direction, the right direction. It was almost like I was being "tempted" to trust God, to believe that I was going to be okay despite the financial hit.

I prayed, "God, what do I do?" I felt like he directed me to get out of bed. So I did. I turned on the light and pulled a book off my shelf called *Foxe's Book of Martyrs*.

It's a compilation of stories about incredible women and men of God who died torturous deaths simply because they were followers of Jesus. I read story after story of real suffering, all in the name of Christ. As I read, the Bible verses I had memorized crept into my mind. The declarations I had said so many times started echoing in my mind.

> Money is not and never will be a problem for me.
> My God is an abundant provider who meets every need.
> Because I am blessed, I will always be a blessing.
> I will lead the way with irrational generosity, because I know it's truly more blessed to give than to receive.

Suddenly my temporary financial tax hit just went away. I realized in a visceral way what I already knew in my head: that my security is not in money but in God alone. More money doesn't give me more peace; more trust in God's goodness does. That's exactly what happened as I sat there reading the book; I was flooded with peace.

I realized I hadn't quite achieved automaticity yet, but I had created a new pathway. A trench of truth was cutting into my thought process regarding money.

Now, years later, I can honestly say I'm not triggered the way I was for decades. Rather than focusing on saving more money, I'm consumed with giving more. Don't get me wrong. I've got other issues I'm working on. But I'm thankful to say my faith is now bigger than my financial fears. My declaration is no longer just words on a page. I own those words now. God's truth is in my heart. Not just something I read but something I live.

You can have that happen too. Let God help you rewire your brain and renew your mind. You will change your thinking and change your life.

--- EXERCISE 6 ---

LEARNING TO RUMINATE

TODAY'S EXERCISE IS STRAIGHTFORWARD: CHOOSE A verse or passage, possibly one you found for a truth in exercise 5, and practice ruminating and meditating as I taught you in this chapter.

A few helpful suggestions for this process are:

1. Look intently at each word and phrase, one at a time. Don't make any assumptions or skip a single word. Each one is important to the overall meaning for you.

2. Type your Scripture reference into your search engine and look for online Bible commentaries. Read what some of the great theologians have had to say about the meanings of the Hebrew or Greek words used in your verse or passage. This level of personal study can bring new meaning and connotation as you work to apply the truth in your life.

3. Ask God, the author of the Word, to speak to your heart about anything specific he might want to say to you through your verse or passage.

My verse or passage:

PART 3

THE REFRAME
PRINCIPLE

Reframe Your Mind, Restore Your Perspective

Trust in the LORD with all your heart,
and do not lean on your own
understanding.
In all your ways acknowledge him,
and he will make straight your paths.

—PROVERBS 3:5–6 ESV

CHAPTER 7

LENSES AND FILTERS

MY WIFE, AMY, AND I HAD JUST GONE OUT ON A ROMANTIC date night. A nice dinner, meaningful conversation, quality time. Now we were home and the kids were in bed or otherwise occupied. We were alone. The mood was right. Amy looked at me with big eyes and said, in her sexiest voice, "Craig, what's wrong with you? You look horrible! Your coloring is all off. Your face is discolored!"

First, I realized that was not her sexy voice.

Second, I thought, *This is not heading in the direction I was expecting.*

Third, I wondered, *Could it be her new glasses?*

Amy had visited the optometrist not long before, and she had picked up her new prescription specs that afternoon. I said, "Amy, maybe try taking off your glasses."

She removed the new frames from her beautiful face, looked at me, and smiled. "Wow! You look good again."

Praise the Lord! She once was blind but now she can see!

"Well, as good as you ever do."

I'll take it.

We discovered that Amy couldn't see me correctly because she was looking at me through defective lenses. Her new glasses made it impossible for her to see reality the way reality really is.

What if we have a similar problem? What if we're looking at the world through defective lenses? We won't be able to see reality the way reality really is.

Imagine you go to a party with a friend. Just before you both walk into the house, your friend grabs you, looks you in the eye, and says, "You do know that everyone at this party thinks you're an idiot, right? For real . . . Alright, let's go!" You're shocked. You had no idea anyone thought of you that way, much less everyone at this party.

Everything at the party would seem different to you.

If the host forgets to take your coat, you know why. She thinks you're an idiot and wants you to leave!

If you see two people whispering and laughing, you know what they're talking about. What an idiot you are!

If your friend decides to leave early, you know what's going on. He's embarrassed to be seen with such an idiot!

You leave the party and your friend says, "Did you believe that whole idiot thing I told you?" You give him a confused look. He smirks and lights up. "Gotcha!"

No one actually thought you were an idiot, but because you assumed they did, you looked at everything through that lens. Remember, a lie believed as truth will affect your life as if it were true. We could say a lens with a distorted view will make lies seem like they're true.

I wonder how often you see what you expect instead of what's really there—reality the way reality really is.

I'M NOT BIASED. YOU'RE BIASED!

Social psychologists have a name for our distorted lenses. They call it a cognitive bias. The term refers to a standardized, consistent pattern of deviating from reality in how we see and process things. If you have a cognitive bias, you create a subjective reality. That construction of your reality, not actual reality, will dictate how you respond and behave in the world.[5]

That's a kind of scholarly way of thinking about cognitive bias, but you don't need that explanation. You see people with a cognitive bias all the time.

You might have a boss who gives the same feedback in the same way to two employees. One receives it as fair, constructive criticism. "That really helped me see a flaw in how I'm doing my job. I appreciate the feedback. This will improve my job performance."

The other person is totally offended. "Who is she to come in here and say any of that? Who does she think she is? You want some feedback? I'll give you some feedback!"

What is the difference? Cognitive bias.

Perhaps the second person had a demanding, insulting parent and now sees every authority figure through that lens.

Two people walk into the same worship service together. The first believes Christians are hypocrites and churches are always out for your money, especially megachurches, where it's "all about numbers."

The second would tell you Christians are not perfect but they're trying, and most mean well. She believes that God is alive and at work in all kinds of churches.

Those two people will experience the exact same service but have very different experiences. Why? It's not the facts that differ but the filter.

Studies show that cognitive bias can impact a person's view of God. Your relationship with your earthly father often colors how you perceive your heavenly Father. If you had a good dad who was involved and full of compassion, it will be easier to view God as relational and caring about the details of your life. If you had a father who was absent or abusive, you are more likely to think of God as distant and disinterested. Same God. Different filter.

You can recognize cognitive bias in others, but can you in yourself?

Part of the problem is that we tend not to see our own cognitive biases. Because if we knew it was a bias, we wouldn't have one.

That's why it's so important to think about what you think about. You cannot defeat an enemy you cannot define. Ask probing questions to explore why you think what you think.

As I've practiced these disciplines over the past few years, I've discovered my cognitive bias toward believing I'm not enough and needing to prove myself. And toward thinking that I don't have enough and need to get more to provide financial security.

> **THAT'S WHY IT'S SO IMPORTANT TO THINK ABOUT WHAT YOU THINK ABOUT. YOU CANNOT DEFEAT AN ENEMY YOU CANNOT DEFINE.**

What about you? How does your cognitive bias block your path to progress? More important, what are you going to do about it?

Let's work to define our cognitive biases so we can defeat them.

CONTROL FREAK

Hi, my name is Craig and I am a control freak.

That's not a cognitive bias; that's just a fact. When I say I'm controlling, I mean that I am *controlling*. Come to my house and check out who's holding the remote control. I am. If our TV is on, I have the remote. Why? Because God ordained me to handle this special spiritual calling. My family wants to watch what's on, but only I have the God-given gift of caring more about what *else* might be on. Because God's favor is upon me, we are able to watch twelve to fourteen shows at one time. Why? Because I am in control of the remote control.

Get in a car with me and see who's driving. I am. Does not matter who else is in the car or whose car it is. I'm driving. Yes, I will drive you in your car. And if for some end-of-times, sign-of-the-apocalypse reason someone else is driving the car, there is a good chance I will grab the steering wheel from my seat and take over. You think I'm kidding? I'm not kidding. Because I'm controlling.

Are there some ways in which you're controlling? How would your family or friends answer that for you? Perhaps you use reverse psychology on your kids, drop not-so-subtle hints to your spouse about your expectations for your anniversary, or humble-brag to your boss to make sure you get credit for work he didn't know about. Those are all control issues.

Here's the problem: being in control is an illusion.

I don't like to admit this, but I cannot control what has happened to me, and I cannot control what will happen to me.

Neither can you. No matter how hard you try, you cannot control what's happened in the past or what will happen in the future. That's bad news, but there is good news.

You cannot control what's happened or what will happen, but you can control how you perceive it.

Social psychologists have a name for taking control of how we perceive things. They call it cognitive reframing.[6] It's when we learn to identify and correct irrational thinking. We could say this happens when we unbias our bias.

Our frame is how we view things. It's the cognitive bias through which we look at and interpret what's happening. Reframing is when we decide we are not going to hang on to old perceptions that have worked against us. We are going to choose a different, more godly, more productive way of thinking.

Experts in the psychotherapeutic world share steps that help us to reframe, to take control of our thoughts and overcome our cognitive bias, such as:

- *Stay calm.* If you react, you will probably react the way you've always reacted.
- *Identify the situation.* What exactly, and truly, is happening?
- *Identify your automatic thoughts.* If something at my house breaks and I know it will be an expensive repair, my automatic response is to panic just a little bit. But while I cannot control what breaks, I can control how I perceive it. So instead of just thinking my automatic thought, I identify that thought. I can take it captive and make it obedient to Christ. Then I take an additional step:
- *Find objective supportive evidence.* I want to deal in reality, and so I search for objective data on which to base my thinking, such as: Things are going to break. They always do eventually. That's why you have an emergency fund. Just call someone to get it fixed. There is no reason to freak out.

You can take these same steps. You cannot control what happens to you, but you *can* control how you frame it.

The GOAT (greatest of all time) of reframing was the apostle Paul.

Paul had a strategic plan for advancing the gospel—go to Rome. If he could get to Rome and preach Jesus to the leaders there, the city could become a launchpad to spread the gospel all over the world.

> **❝ YOU CANNOT CONTROL WHAT HAPPENS TO YOU, BUT YOU *CAN* CONTROL HOW YOU FRAME IT. ❞**

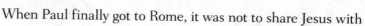

When Paul finally got to Rome, it was not to share Jesus with government officials. He went there as a prisoner. He was locked up under house arrest, chained to a rotating contingent of guards, awaiting a possible execution. Paul prayed for an opportunity, but it was not happening.

Paul's circumstances were out of his control. Circumstances are almost always out of our control.

You've been where Paul was.

You thought, *If I just get this degree, I will get that job.* You got the degree, but you did not get the job.

You planned on being married by now, but you have not found Mr. or Mrs. Right.

Or you did find and marry the right person, but everything went wrong. This is not the way life was supposed to go.

You've been praying for years for your prodigal child, but God has not answered that prayer.

Paul was in that same situation—circumstances he did not want and could not control. He wrote to the church at Philippi about what was happening to him. What might he have said? He could have written, "Now, I want you to know, brothers and sisters, that what has happened to me really sucks. I wanted to spread the good news through preaching to government officials, but that did not happen. As a result of this hell I've been through, I have decided prayer doesn't work, and I am never going back to church again."

But that is not what Paul wrote. Could have been, but no. Remember, Paul couldn't control what happened to him, but he could control how he framed it. Here's what he actually wrote to the Philippians: "I want you to know, my dear brothers and sisters, that everything that has happened to me here has helped to spread the Good News. For everyone here, including the whole palace guard, knows that I am in chains because of Christ. And because of my imprisonment, most of the believers here have gained confidence and boldly speak God's message without fear" (Phil. 1:12–14 NLT).

Paul was saying, "I had a plan, but God had a better plan! This is a whole different way to advance the gospel than what I was thinking. God has blessed me with prison guards who are chained to me. They have no choice but to listen to me tell them about Jesus! These soldiers have the ear of influential leaders! And, get this, every eight hours they chain a new guard to me! And they think I'm the prisoner. Ha! God is moving. I can't wait to see what he does next!"

You cannot control what happens to you, but you can control how you frame it.

The third tool to change your thinking is the Reframe Principle: Reframe your mind, restore your perspective. (The first tool is the Replacement Principle: Remove the lies, replace with truth. The second tool is the Rewire Principle: Rewire your brain, renew your mind.) Reframing has changed my thinking and changed my life.

Reframing your past—and preframing your future—will change your life.

——— EXERCISE 7 ———

COGNITIVE BIAS, CONTROL, AND REFRAMING

COGNITIVE BIAS CAN BE DIFFICULT FOR ANY OF US TO identify in our own lives. But looking for these areas and becoming aware of our thoughts and beliefs to this degree can help us win the war in our minds.

In this exercise, write down any biases or places of control that you may have thought of as you read the chapter. Consider talking with a spouse, loved one, or friend and asking them to help you identify some of these they may see in you. You aren't inviting criticism; you're looking for the opportunity to remove blind spots and grow. Finally, pray, think, and write down any potential ways you can reframe your biases or areas of control.

My cognitive biases:

Areas of control regarding people, places, or circumstances:

Ways I can reframe biases and control issues:

CHAPTER 8

WHAT GOD DIDN'T DO

BACK WHEN I WAS IN MIDDLE SCHOOL, AT THE ROLLER-
skating rink the DJ would crank songs by the J. Geils Band. A
huge sing-along-while-you-skate J. Geils hit was "Freeze-Frame."
The song featured such Shakespearean-level lyrics as "It's like the
freeze, she's breeze." The song was about savoring a moment so
much that you want to stay in it forever.

There are special moments in life we would love to stay in
forever.

There are sad moments in life that we can get stuck in forever.
They are not the moments we want to freeze-frame, but too often
we do. Those formative moments can become the lens through
which we view what happens for the rest of our lives. They form
our cognitive bias, the frame we use to define our reality. We
need to unfreeze our frames. We need to go back and rewrite the
narrative we have been telling ourselves.

So how do we reframe our past?

We thank God for what he didn't do.

We look for God's goodness.

This is the shortest chapter in the book, but it might be one of the most powerful. Here's why: it will reframe your past. Thanking God for what he's done is easy for most of us. But I've learned to also thank God for what he didn't do.

> **WE NEED TO UNFREEZE OUR FRAMES. WE NEED TO GO BACK AND REWRITE THE NARRATIVE WE HAVE BEEN TELLING OURSELVES.**

To discover those blessings can take a long time, but when you finally have that aha moment—wow! Here's an example from my life.

My dad played professional baseball. I was born and bred to be a professional baseball player. Most infants are given milk and Cheerios. I was given Gatorade and sunflower seeds.

With good baseball genes and great baseball coaching, I seemed to have a real future in pro ball. Until the accident.

I was in eighth grade. My baseball team was the best in our league. We made it to the championship, and our coach told me I would be the starting pitcher in the big game.

The night before, we went to a batting cage. Normally I would hit in the one that was appropriate for my age. This night I was feeling like a big-timer, like the result of a scientific experiment combining the genes of George Brett and Mike Schmidt and Wade Boggs. Yes, I was George Schmoggs. I decided to go to the batting cage with the fastest pitch, meant for college-level players and semipro wannabes. But I was sure I was ready. I thought, *King Kong or Barry Bonds ain't got nothing on me.*

The first pitch was inside and, before I could get out of the way, crushed my pitching hand against the bat. My fingers were broken, shattered into pieces.

Needless to say, I did not pitch the next day. I could not play for a long time.

Baseball was everything to me, so I felt like my life had been shattered as badly as my hand. I could not understand how God could let something like this happen to me. Inside I was in a rage.

Then our family moved to another city. When you're a teenager, moving stinks. Losing your friends and having to make new ones is not fun. Not only did we move; we moved to Ardmore, Oklahoma. Want to know what Ardmore is known for? If you are driving from Dallas, Texas, to Oklahoma City, Ardmore is where you stop to go to the bathroom. That's right. We moved to the pit stop town.

When we moved to Ardmore, it was not baseball season. It was tennis season. *Tennis? No thanks.* I knew nothing about tennis, except that this Andre Agassi guy seemed to have cool hair and wore jean shorts in his matches. I was not interested in playing tennis.

Except . . . there was a cute girl on the tennis team. So, tennis? *Sure, I'll play tennis.*

Just to be clear, this was not the cute exchange student from France. This was three years before her. The tennis player was just a normal, cute Oklahoma girl. Since I could not speak French and did not yet have an awesome Buick with a spoiler, I would have to impress her with my tennis playing ability. Except I had never played tennis. Still, I tried out and, amazingly, I made the team.

Six people qualified to compete on the traveling team. I was number six, the last guy to make the team. When baseball season came around, my plan was to drop tennis and go back to the sport I loved. But the thought of having pitches coming at me brought back memories of having my fingers broken. So I decided that taking a year off would be good for me. I stuck with tennis, and we placed second in the state that year.

The next season a few guys had graduated and I had improved, so I somehow ended up winning the number one spot on the team. That year we won the state championship. I kept playing tennis through the rest of high school.

After graduation I received a full-ride tennis scholarship to a college I never would have gone to otherwise. That college is where I fell deep into sin and where I met Jesus in a life-changing way. A lot of people started making fun of me for being a Jesus freak. One day a girl said, "You are so weird for Jesus. There's a girl at another school who's weird for Jesus like you. Her name is Amy. You two should meet and get married."

That is exactly what happened. Boom!

And why did that happen?

Because of what God didn't do. He didn't answer my prayer to protect me and prepare me for the championship baseball game. Because of what God didn't do, I got a full scholarship in tennis, a sport I never planned on playing, at a college I never planned on going to, where I met Jesus and my wife!

A few years later Amy and I started Life.Church. We also started having babies. A lot of them.

Thanking God for what he didn't do. Here's another story.

PASTORAL PARADIGM SHIFT

Amy went into labor with Sam, our fourth of six, at five o'clock on a Sunday morning. I faced what seemed like an impossible choice. I had preached the night before in our Saturday night service. There was now no way I could be there to preach without deserting Amy and missing my son's birth, neither of which I wanted to do. It was too late to ask anyone else to speak for me. We didn't know what to do. I wondered, *Why, God? Why couldn't this baby be born on any other day at any other time?*

Feeling desperate, we decided to show the video of the sermon from the Saturday night service. Our team thought people would forgive us for showing Saturday night's teaching on the screen, hoping they would understand, since Amy and I were at the hospital having a baby.

We showed the video, and people didn't seem to even notice! The response was great. Even more people came to Christ than on a usual Sunday. We started wondering, *Wait, could video sermons work as a strategy? Could we start new church locations and show the message on video?*

Today, Life.Church has more than thirty-five campuses meeting in eleven states. Tens of thousands of people are impacted by the gospel all over the country, and hundreds of thousands globally, through Church Online.

Why?

Because God didn't answer my prayer that Sam would be born on a different day of the week at a different time. Our son was born on a Sunday morning to a woman I met because God didn't answer my prayer to become a professional baseball player, and instead sent me to a college on a tennis scholarship.

I am so thankful for what God didn't do in my life.

Isn't the same true for you? Think about some of the things you've wanted and prayers you've prayed. Aren't you so glad God didn't do what you hoped he would?

Think about some of the worst circumstances you've had to go through. You never would have chosen them, and maybe you prayed God would pull you out of them, but didn't they help you grow in ways that are crucial to who you are today?

Think about some of the best parts of your life right now. Aren't some of them things you never imagined or planned for, but were just serendipitous shooting stars flung into your life by the Father of the heavenly lights?

> **SOMETIMES WE NEED TO THANK GOD FOR WHAT HE DIDN'T DO. DEVELOPING THAT DISCIPLINE HELPS US REFRAME OUR PAST.**

Sometimes we need to thank God for what he didn't do. Developing that discipline helps us reframe our past.

Why? Here's why: "'My thoughts are not your thoughts, neither are your ways my ways,' declares the LORD. 'As the heavens are higher than the earth, so are my ways higher than your ways and my thoughts than your thoughts'" (Isa. 55:8–9).

We are wise when we trust that he is working even when we

aren't aware of it. We are also wise when we trust the way he's working, even when it isn't the way we want. Because instead of feeling like a victim of random circumstances in a chaotic world, you see that you have a God who has protected you, often from yourself, in ways you didn't realize.

It only makes sense: If God knows more than we do (and he does), then certainly there will be times when we ask for things that he knows are not good for us. In his goodness, then, he says no to those requests. The problem is that we never think we're asking for something that isn't good for us. I knew that I needed to play baseball in high school. And God was gracious enough to say no.

Now when I think about stepping into that batting cage, I have a perspective that's different from the one I had a week after my bones shattered. What happened that day remains the same, but the meaning has been changed by the reframe.

——— EXERCISE 8 ———
UNANSWERED PRAYERS

THINK BACK THROUGH YOUR LIFE ON YOUR PAST HOPES, dreams, desires, and relationships. Think through some what-ifs in a positive, good way. See if you can come up with situations, much like the two personal examples I gave you, from your life in which God didn't answer your prayer or allow your dreams to come true. See these situations through the filter that he knew all along what was best for you. This can be an amazing and eye-opening glimpse into the deep love your heavenly Father has for you.

God, in my life, I thank you that you didn't:

CHAPTER 9

COLLATERAL GOODNESS

HOW DO WE REFRAME OUR PAST?

We thank God for what he didn't do.

We look for God's goodness.

We practice gratitude for the consequences of God's activity in our lives.

You've heard the term "collateral damage"? Think of this as God's collateral goodness.

Like any good habit, looking for God's collateral goodness requires practice.

If you look for what's bad, you will find the bad. If you look for what's negative, you will find plenty to be negative about. If you look for things to be critical of, there is always going to be something to criticize.

On the other hand, if you look for God's goodness, you will see it. You'll start seeing his fingerprints and occasionally feel like he's winking at you. As you pay attention to how God is working, you will also find yourself seeing the good in people. This practice will change your relationships. Your attitude will be transformed, and the right attitude always precedes the right actions.

There's a story about a young man who was at a crisis point about his future and didn't know what direction to turn. His mom told him he should go visit a retired pastor who for many years had lived just a few houses down. Barely knowing the man but desperate for help, he agreed. As the discussion finally turned toward faith, the young man said, "The problem I have is I just can't seem to see God in this world." The elder pastor responded quietly yet confidently, "Well, son, I have a very different problem. When I look at the same world, I cannot *not* see him."

You find what you are looking for.

Unfortunately for me, looking for God's goodness has been a struggle. Negativity and lack of gratitude has been another stronghold in my life. Again, this is me just being real.

I hate to admit this now, but for years I complained to my wife, "I don't have a life." I'd whine, "Amy, I have to work every weekend while everyone else is out having fun. And I even have to work holidays! Everyone else is off on holidays. And I can't go out in public and play with my kids at the park, because so many people there know me from our church. And I also have a big family, and my bathroom doesn't even have a door on it. I haven't gone to the bathroom alone in years. I don't have a life." I'd grumble, "All I do is church and family, family and church. Church and family, family and church. I just don't have a life."

One day Amy looked at me (she had new lenses by then) and said—sincerely, not sarcastically—"I am so sad for you." I thought, *Yeah, it is sad that I don't have a life!* But she continued: "I'm sad for you because all I have is church and family. That's my life too. And I love my life."

Ouch. If you smell smoke right now, that's just my self-pity getting scorched.

I thought about it and realized that if you were to rewind the clock fifteen years and ask me to design my life, I couldn't come up with anything as good as my reality. I could not have picked a wife as amazing as Amy. I could not have imagined so many great kids running around my house. I could not have dreamed up a church so incredible. I have the greatest, most blessed life of anyone I know. And hey, going to the bathroom alone is overrated anyway.

In that moment after Amy's gut-level honesty, I decided to take my *I don't have a life* thought captive and make it obedient to Christ. We find what we are looking for, and we reframe by looking for God's goodness.

> **WE FIND WHAT WE ARE LOOKING FOR, AND WE REFRAME BY LOOKING FOR GOD'S GOODNESS.**

I decided I would look for his goodness and be grateful. Of course, the change wasn't immediate. But over time the reframe worked! Searching for God's goodness transformed my attitude. I stopped feeling sorry for myself and started feeling satisfied, even amazed at the life God gave me.

Except for Mondays. I loved my life except for Mondays.

IT'S FRIDAY, BUT MONDAY'S COMING

I have grueling weekends. On Saturdays I go into spiritual lockdown. Much like an athlete on game day, I focus my energy on getting into a zone for the message I will be preaching Saturday and Sunday in our church services. When I'm preaching to our church, I get very intense. I become spiritually in tune to what God is saying and doing and where he is working. When I look at people, I'm locking eyes with them. It's a little scary! Then I preach, multiple times in multiple services, which is both exhilarating and draining.

Finally, by Sunday afternoon, I come crashing down.

On Mondays, I'm still mostly dead and just trying to recover. Mondays are often dark days. My head hurts. I'm in a fog. I can't make wise decisions. So I came to the conclusion a long time ago that I just have to endure Mondays. The valley of Mondays is the price I pay for mountaintop Saturdays and Sundays.

One particular Monday I was up early, doing my daily Bible study. Not because I wanted to but just because I'm supposed to. I read a verse that I had read at least a hundred times. But this was the first time I had read it on a Monday. Psalm 118:24: "This is the day that the LORD has made; let us rejoice and be glad in it" (ESV). Yet this time I didn't read the verse; the verse read me. I realized Mondays are from God. He made them. I did not have to frame every Monday as a bad day. I could "rejoice and be glad in it." After all, God made Mondays just as he had the other six days.

I decided to reframe my Mondays, starting that day. On my

drive to work, all the way, I made my new declaration using this freshly applied truth from God's Word: "This is the day the Lord has made. I will rejoice. I will be glad in it. I will look for God's good hand. I will see his favor at work."

Guess what happened? That Monday was a better day. Not perfect but better. Ever since, I have reframed Mondays by looking for God's goodness, and Mondays just keep getting better.

We find what we are looking for, and we reframe by looking for God's goodness.

Once again, I want to be real with you: this is not easy. Well, I can say it's not been easy for me. Sure, I make progress, but there is always something pulling me back to my old way of thinking. That's the nature of a stronghold; demolishing them takes divine power and continual mental discipline. And some fall far more slowly than others. I've often found that when I think I have victory and the battle is won, there's still battling left to do.

DIVINE DELIVERY

This became a reality to me again when my book *Hope in the Dark* came out. That book is especially close to my heart because I tell of the pain my family has been through. I was so excited for the book to release, believing it could help people find hope and healing from their hurts.

After release day, *Hope in the Dark* sold out in two days. The physical copy of the book was not available for the next month! You might think, *Oh, well, praise God, Craig, that your book sold so well.* No, not me. I was upset that the printers could not keep up with the demand. I knew there were people who wanted to read the book but could not get it. I was convinced that the lack of availability would stall momentum. I was not looking for God's goodness; I was just plain upset.

But then I heard about Rance and Heather. Heather, who was in her thirties, had been sick with significant physical issues. She almost died, spent three months in the hospital, but then recovered. She went back home to Rance and their son, Boston, but soon got sick again. One day Rance found Heather unresponsive, and she never regained consciousness. She died at the young age of thirty-eight. Turns out Heather had ordered a book on Amazon that was not available but was finally delivered the week between her death and the funeral.

Her husband, Rance, opened the package when it arrived and found a book, *Hope in the Dark: Believing God Is Good When Life Is Not*. Rance, who just lost his wife and was left to raise his son alone, who had to be questioning why God would let this happen, thought, *Wow. God is still with me. He cares so much about me, he had this book delivered to me at the perfect time.*

Even in the midst of something terrible happening, there was God's collateral goodness. And to Rance's credit, because he was looking for God, he could see him when he saw the book title.

I thought the book being out of stock was the worst possible outcome. I had prayed God would get the books out to people quickly. But God's timing is perfect. Once again I had to thank

God for what he didn't do, and realize that I had been ignoring God's goodness.

Do you need to reframe your past? Do you need to thank God for what he didn't do, and start looking for his goodness?

You could be set free. Free from being haunted by things you have done and things that were done to you. Free from mindsets that have kept you shackled to your past. Free from ruts of self-defeating habits.

Wouldn't you like to be free? You can. Reframe your life, and experience the blessings of God's collateral goodness.

PREFRAME YOUR FUTURE

You will always find what you are looking for.

Think about the difference between a vulture and a hummingbird.

Vultures soar high in the sky, searching. What does a vulture find? Dead things. The ugly, oversized bird doesn't stop until he finds lifeless roadkill. Vultures can sniff out a dead critter from more than a mile away and have been known to cruise thirty to fifty miles in search of rotting food.

Now contrast the vulture to the tiny hummingbird. With wings flapping twenty beats a second, this small bird finds what? Not dead, disgusting, rancid meat but sweet, life-giving nectar.

Daily, each bird finds what it is looking for.

The same is true for you. You will always find what you are looking for.

> **WHEN WE REFRAME WHAT HAPPENED IN OUR YESTERDAYS, THAT CHANGES OUR TODAYS.**

When we reframe what happened in our yesterdays, that changes our todays. We are able to experience life without the old, negative cognitive bias and start seeing through the lens of God's goodness.

Just as we can reframe, we can also preframe.

Preframing is choosing how I will view something before it happens. Instead of getting there and letting my old way of looking at things take over, leading me to interpret what might be positive as negative, I proactively choose the frame I will use to evaluate my experience.

I first learned to preframe from my high school tennis coach. As I mentioned before, early in my tennis career I went to the state championship. Somehow I was in the quarter finals, playing against Mandi Ochoa. He was a senior. I was a sophomore. He was a legend. I was a nobody. He was ranked fourth in the state. I was ranked nothing. Apparently, they didn't have enough numbers to rank someone like me.

But as we played, I had him against the ropes! We split sets. The crowd was getting hyped. You could hear them murmuring, "Who's this little kid about to dethrone Mandi Ochoa? Did you see the spoiler and eagles on his cool brown car? This unranked kid could win the state championship! He was cranking Duran Duran when he drove in. He is hungry like the wolf! But why did he have his headlights on in the middle of the afternoon?"

I had Ochoa down five games to one in the final set. The game count was 40–love. One more point and victory would be mine.

In the final set, I had seven match points. Match point means that if you win the point, you win the whole match. Seven times I had match points! Seven opportunities to knock off the number-four-ranked player in the state!

I lost all seven. I was up five games to one in the third set, and I lost seven to five.

I was nicknamed Craig Gro-choke-el. In Oklahoma, people started saying, "If the matches get tight, Craig will lose. He's Craig Gro-choke-el."

You may want to take note of that. It's pretty significant. The frame through which you look at the world may not be one you picked up on your own. Sometimes other people force the frame on you.

- Your father said you would never amount to anything.
- Your mother made you feel unattractive and overweight even when you lost weight.
- Kids at school told you to just accept the fact that you were a loser.
- A grandparent insisted only rich people are important.

Maybe you have a cognitive bias constructed by other people. You accepted what they told you as truth, and even though it was a lie, ever since it has affected your life as if it were true.

When everyone in the Oklahoma tennis circuit started saying, "Craig chokes in big matches," my coach decided to put a stop to what he knew would only limit me. He looked me in the eyes and said, "No! That is not true, Craig. Do not own that label." He explained, "You now have more experience that will help you succeed than anyone else. You have been in that tight spot. You know what doesn't work. You know that when people get nervous in sports, most start playing not to lose. You need to play to win. Instead of not taking risks, you need to push harder, swing harder. You will be better because you lost. From now on you will use your experience to rise to the occasion and win."

From that day on I have told myself, *Groeschel, you are a pressure player. You are at your best when things are at their worst. In those moments, your God is for you and your God is with you.*

My declaration for tennis became one for pressure situations in life. In leadership, the tougher the circumstances, the more I want to be involved. If there's a spiritual situation, if someone is about to die who doesn't know Christ, let me be the one to have the conversation. Why? I have preframed the outcome. I will walk into it knowing that my God is for me and with me. I will not play to lose. I will play to win. I am a pressure player. I rise to the occasion.

That's not just what I tell myself. That's how I live and handle those tough moments. Because I can't control what happens to me. But I can control how I frame it. And the way I frame it will dictate how I respond and behave.

How do you need to preframe your future?

What situations do you know you will be walking into?

What would be the most positive, life-building, God-honoring, mutually edifying way for you to approach that moment?

Preframe it. With God's help you can choose the frame through which you will step into that situation.

Let's say you wake up knowing you are facing an overwhelmingly busy day. Instead of complaining about how hard it will be, preframe it with a more positive, godly perspective. Tell yourself, *Today I get to experience God's strength when I am weak. He gives me everything I need to do what he's called me to do. Rather than a busy, bad day, I'm going to have a positive, productive one.*

If you are nervous about the challenging conversation you need to have with a friend, try to preframe it with faith. Instead of imagining a blowup, thank God ahead of time for your friend and for giving you the words to say. Decide you are going to do the right thing and trust God with the results.

Let's say you have an intimidating doctor's appointment later in the week. Your fears might be overwhelming as you forecast the worst possible outcome. Instead choose a different frame for your future. Believe God has heard your prayers and that you will hear good news from the doctor. And if you don't, remind yourself that God is always good. Collaterally good. No matter what you face, he will be with you. You can't control what happens, but you can control how you frame it.

Know that there's a different way to look at the world. We can choose to make our cognitive bias the goodness of God. We can look at our circumstances through the lens of his mercy and grace. There is not a moment when we have been forsaken or forgotten.

We can't control what happens to us, but we can control how we frame the outcome, even before it happens.

—— EXERCISE 9 ——

YOUR COLLATERAL GOODNESS

In your life, is there a circumstance or a relationship that you know God allowed you to begin to see from a different perspective, so that you changed your attitude from negative to positive, from harmful to healthy? What happened to change your mindset?

Recalling my personal example, ask yourself, "What in my life right now is the Monday—the relationship or circumstance in which I struggle to see anything positive or good?" Write it out.

What is one practical step you could take to change your mind about this situation?

What would you want to see God do to change this situation?

What would be the most positive, life-building, God-honoring, mutually edifying way for you to approach this situation?

YOU CAN USE THIS EXERCISE TO CONTINUE TO REFRAME circumstances in your life and open doors for God to give you a new perspective. Remember, you can't control what happens to you, but you can control how you frame it. And the way you frame it will dictate how you respond and behave.

PART 4

THE REJOICE PRINCIPLE

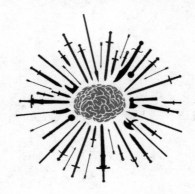

Revive Your Soul, Reclaim Your Life

Praise the LORD.

Give thanks to the LORD, for he is good;
his love endures forever.

—PSALM 106:1

CHAPTER 10

PROBLEMS, PANIC,

AND PRESENCE

BLUE VANS, MAN. BLUE VANS FREAK ME OUT. IF ONE DRIVES by, my heart beats fast and I'm ready to rush the driver or run for my life.

Why?

When I was a kid, my dad was driving our family home after dinner at our favorite hole-in-the-wall burger joint. Another driver who did not approve of my father's post burger-fries-and-shake driving followed us to our house. We pulled into our driveway, and a blue van screeched in right behind us. Like a scene from an action movie.

A very angry guy got out of the van, screaming. He strung together a combination of four-letter words that would make a drunk fraternity boy blush. The man came running toward our car, nostrils flared, eyes wide, fists clenched, and lunged at my dad.

Bad decision. My dad can hold his own, and the man soon ran back to his blue van, in one piece only by the grace of God.

That night my mother sat me down in the living room and explained in no uncertain terms that there was a man out there who was extremely angry with my father and probably our entire family. This man now knew where we lived, and he drove a blue van. She warned me, "If you ever see a blue van, run inside, lock the doors, and call the police."

My mom's loving yet stern warning felt much like my grandma's prophecy about another financial depression. So another pattern of fear emerged. For years, every time I saw a blue van, I would run inside, lock the doors, and hide under my bed. Just like Mom told me to do.

To this day I go into high alert if I see a blue van. A blue van is a threat and pushes my panic button.

I bet you have some threats that lead you to panic. They may be a little irrational, like my aversion to blue vans. Or they may be very real.

What perceived threats cause you to panic? Not being able to control your future? A bad grade? The scale saying you've gained five pounds? Someone giving you a funny look? A friend who takes their time in replying to your text or doesn't respond at all? Your preteen texting with a member of the opposite sex? Traffic on the way to work? A conversation with your mom revealing she's farther into dementia? Your boss walking through the office? The thought that you might fail?

We've said that your life will always move in the direction of your strongest thoughts. That's good news if you are thinking on things that are noble, right, pure, lovely, admirable, excellent, or praiseworthy. It's bad news if you are thinking on things that are dishonorable, false, ugly, anxious, unjust, fearful, or just plain irrational.

Our runaway negative thoughts can spiral out of control and lead our lives in the wrong direction.

> **❝ OUR RUNAWAY NEGATIVE THOUGHTS CAN SPIRAL OUT OF CONTROL AND LEAD OUR LIVES IN THE WRONG DIRECTION. ❞**

So why do we panic?

There is a little, almond-shaped part of our brains called the amygdala. The amygdala is responsible for emotions and survival instincts. When you're afraid, the amygdala lights up like a pinball machine, producing a fight-or-flight response. The amygdala deploys a tsunami of adrenaline, preparing the body for action.

That's a good thing if you are hiking a trail and come across a poisonous snake poised to strike. You need to get out of its way quickly. The amygdala did its job.

It's also a good thing if you are driving and suddenly a cow comes flying at your windshield. (I live in Oklahoma, where we average fifty-two tornados a year and have lots of farms, so yes, this could happen.) You must react immediately, choosing either to fight the cow (good luck with that!) or to take flight from the cow (my suggestion). When you swerve and the cow soars by, you have your amygdala to thank for staying alive.

The problem is that the amygdala is not objective. The way it responds to a hurtling cow is the same way it responds to a hurtful conversation. The way it responds to a noise letting you know a burglar has broken into your house is the same way it responds to a notification letting you know your bank account is overdrawn.

If you are confronted with an angry bovine or an aggressive burglar, you need the adrenaline to spark your body into action. If you are facing a disappointing text or a disagreeable spouse, you do not need the adrenaline, and it will just loiter in your body, acting as an unwanted hype man. You will feel stressed, agitated, on edge. Can you spell P-A-N-I-C?

What makes you panic? How about I confess mine, and perhaps you'll feel comfortable admitting yours.

MANIC PANIC

Before I unpack what causes me to panic, I want you to know I am not bragging or complaining. I am also not saying my world is more difficult than anyone else's. Everyone has their own stuff, their own issues. My world is not more difficult, just different. You may wish you had my problems and vice versa.

I struggle with what I call content anxiety. A big part of what I do is creating content. With sermons for my church, speeches at conferences, quarterly messages for our staff, episodes for my leadership podcast, and multiple weekly video leadership trainings, I can be working on a dozen messages at once.

Now, not all messages take equal effort. Some of the smaller ones I can prepare relatively quickly. But the bigger ones take from twelve to sixteen hours per message. Occasionally they will demand up to twenty hours.

Working on twelve messages for at least twelve hours per message is, well, a *lot* of hours. I often feel like there are simply not enough hours available to do all the hours of work I need to do. So to try to manufacture more hours, I started to wake up earlier and stay awake later. I'd often get up as early as 3:30 a.m. to study, go all day, and then work after the kids had gone to bed at night.

Contrary to cultural belief, pastors do more than just preach on Sunday. I also have to fit in meetings, train new employees, give pastoral care, and so forth. The demands for my time go on and on.

Yet my stress is not just about hours and workload. I don't just have to write messages; they have to be creative and relevant—all of them. Keeping things fresh is not as easy as it sounds. And here's the reality: every time I read the Bible, nothing in it has changed. The world is created. Adam and Eve sin. The earth floods and the ark floats. The bush burns and the sea parts. Every Christmas, the Virgin Mary has a baby, and his name is Jesus. Every Easter, the tomb is empty.

Don't get me wrong. These truths changed my life. I am honored and humbled to preach the good news every week. I just feel a constant pressure to present the Word in a way that will continue to impact people's lives. Tell the same stories with a new framing. Customize to the ever-changing culture without ever compromising the message.

In 2019 I had to decide on and name a message series for my church. Because of all the prep work our creative and media teams put in for our series, I need to let them know what I'll be speaking on a couple months in advance. I've done this for decades, but this time it just wasn't happening. It seemed like I had finally come to the end of my rope. For the first time in my ministry, I hit a wall. I had no new ideas, no insights into Scripture, no revelation from God, and nothing meaningful to say.

I was empty. I felt scared beyond description. I had to fight to catch my breath. It seemed like the walls were slowly closing in around me. For the first time in more than a quarter of a century as a pastor, I wondered if maybe I had pushed too hard, had nothing left to give, and should just hang it up. Fear gripped me. Panic set in. Life became a massive, confusing, heart-wrenching ball of uncontrollable anxiety.

What was happening? My amygdala went into overdrive, doing double duty, sending adrenaline in a stampede through my body, leaving me in a panic like I had never experienced before.

All right, there is my honest confession. (Did you get a little tense just reading about the way I felt?)

Does my confession make you feel better? Maybe things aren't as bad as you thought! Or you might wonder why you're reading a book on winning the war in your mind by someone so messed up. Either way, I was honest. Now it's your turn.

What about you? Be gut-level honest. What makes you panic?

Whatever that is, your amygdala, which in true fight-or-flight situations is your best friend, is also going to work against you. But wait. You have another portion of your brain that will help your slightly confused amygdala: your prefrontal cortex. The prefrontal cortex is the logical part of the brain.

Think of your amygdala as your twitchy, amped-up, overca-ffeinated, overstimulated, always-on-edge, high-blood-pressure cousin. Think of your prefrontal cortex as your thoughtful, level-headed, realistic, even-tempered uncle with a law degree.

For example, it's the middle of the night. You hear a noise in the house.

Your amygdala screams, "There's someone in the house! He is going to kill you!"

Your prefrontal cortex clears his throat and says, "It was just the cat."

Your amygdala screams louder, "You're gonna die! Grab the baseball bat under the bed! You have to go fight the killer in your house! But you'll still probably die!"

Your prefrontal cortex patiently insists, "If it was a killer, I don't think a bat would help you. Just the cat. Now go back to sleep."

Your amygdala keeps arguing, "The cat isn't that loud! It's not the cat! Jump out the window! It's your only way to survive! Jump! Now!"

Your prefrontal cortex rolls his eyes. "If someone had broken into the house, the alarm would have gone off. Besides, if it was a killer and you did jump out the window, what would happen to your wife and kids?"

Your amygdala yells, "They can fend for themselves! Jump!"

Prefrontal cortex, calmly: "I repeat: it's just the cat."

Amygdala, louder now: "If he's right, then kill the cat!"

I know you have these conversations inside yourself just like I do; they can happen in a matter of seconds while you try to make a decision.

God gave you the logical part of your brain to keep the emotional part of your brain in check. The prefrontal cortex tries to remind me that my bank account is safe and blue vans are not really out to get me, and it tries to assure you that a robber is not breaking into your home. (But you should probably get rid of the cat anyway, since he's building up a big furball to vomit on your couch.)

Despite the help of our prefrontal cortex buddy, we can spend a lot of our time allowing our problems to cause us to panic. What we crave is peace. So what do we do? How do we not plunge into panic and instead find a pathway from problems to peace? I'm so glad you asked. The good news is that our answer is only a prayer away.

NOT IN THE WIND BUT IN THE WHISPER

What causes us to panic?

For me, it's the presence of problems. Typically, it's not just one problem. We start getting into *I'm losing it and I really need a hug* territory when it's problems—plural. Multiple problems. You start feeling like you're playing whack-a-mole. You can handle *an* issue, but when they keep coming, you get to a point where you've had enough. That's when we need to master our minds, fix our thoughts, and worship our God.

Elijah had had enough.

He was a prophet who confronted the evil King Ahab about his sin and prophesied an impending drought. Infuriated, King Ahab threatened to kill Elijah, but the prophet managed to elude his hunter and eventually even confronted 850 false prophets, finally emerging victorious.

With such an incredible triumph, Elijah must have thought that was the end of his problems. But it wasn't. Evil King Ahab had an even more evil wife named Jezebel. She was evil on steroids.

Jezebel decided, *If you want something done right, let a woman do it. My hubby couldn't get rid of Elijah. I'll kill him.*

Elijah realized that even after his great victory, his life was still in danger. He couldn't believe it. It was too much. Elijah was spent. His runaway negative thoughts spiraled out of control and led him into a deep depression. He prayed that he would die.

Notice how irrational that is. His biggest fear was that Jezebel would kill him, so . . . he wanted to die. It doesn't make sense. But Elijah was not thinking clearly. Because he was at the end of his rope. He had hit the wall.

Done. Finished. Broken. Over it. All of it.

Have you been there? Reached the place where you cannot handle one more thing? Your teenager keeps giving you attitude, or you have a series of unplanned expenses, or day after day your boss doesn't recognize your contribution, or your spouse does that thing that annoys you one too many times, and . . . well, you've just had enough.

That's where Elijah was. "I have had enough, LORD," he said. "Take my life, for I am no better than my ancestors who have already died" (1 Kings 19:4 NLT). Notice how he's allowing his negative thoughts to run away and control him. From *I've had enough* to *I'm no better than my ancestors* to *They're lucky because they're already dead.*

I can do the same thing. Can you? From *My life is so hard* to *I can never get it all done* to *I don't like my life* to *No one understands* to *I can't stand all the pressure* to *It's always going to be like this.*

Why? Because of problems. We get fixated on the presence of our problems, and we lose our focus on the presence of God.

God was with Elijah every step of the way, with faithful, visible power and often miraculous provision. Yet when Elijah faced problems, he forgot God.

> **WE GET FIXATED ON THE PRESENCE OF OUR PROBLEMS, AND WE LOSE OUR FOCUS ON THE PRESENCE OF GOD.**

Elijah's name should have been an ever-present reminder of his ever-present God. The *El* in Elijah is short for *Elohim*, which means God. The *i* means "my." *Jah* is a way Israelites shortened *Yahweh*. Yahweh (or Jehovah) is the name of God. Elijah's name meant "Yahweh is my God," yet ironically, he felt God was absent from his life.

Remember the words Paul wrote from prison? "Rejoice in the Lord always. I will say it again: Rejoice! Let your gentleness be evident to all. *The Lord is near.* Do not be anxious about anything, but in every situation, by prayer and petition, with thanksgiving, present your requests to God. And the peace of God, which transcends all understanding, will guard your hearts and your minds in Christ Jesus" (Phil. 4:4–7, emphasis added).

In the middle of trying to help people understand how they can rejoice and experience peace, Paul wrote, "The Lord is near." Recognizing God's presence will give you peace when you have cause for panic.

Elijah forgot that the Lord was near. He needed a reminder. God gave him one. God revealed himself. "The LORD said, 'Go out and stand on the mountain in the presence of the LORD, for the LORD is about to pass by.' Then a great and powerful wind tore the mountains apart and shattered the rocks before the LORD, but the LORD was not in the wind. After the wind there was an earthquake, but the LORD was not in the earthquake. After the earthquake came a fire, but the LORD was not in the fire. And after the fire came a gentle whisper" (1 Kings 19:11–12).

God was not in the wind. God was not in the earthquake. God was not in the fire. Silence, then a whisper. God was in the whisper.

But why would God whisper to Elijah?

When you are overwhelmed and feeling anxious, if you listen for his voice, you'll find that God is whispering to you.

But why? Why does our God whisper?

He whispers because he is so close.

And he whispers to draw us close.

Think about it: When you are sitting next to a loved one and they whisper in your ear, what do you do? You lean into them. And you listen closely.

When we're hurting, when we're afraid, when we're over-whelmed, we may shout up to the heavens and wait for God to shout back. We wish for an audible voice. We don't understand why God doesn't speak loudly to us, commanding our attention in some obvious way. But why doesn't he do this? Why don't you hear him? Perhaps God wants you to slow down, to be still, to listen carefully for his soft, comforting, quiet voice.

Because you have to get quiet and listen intently. God whispers because he is close and because he desires to draw you close. Lean in and listen.

What did Elijah learn on the mountain that day?

When you've had enough, God is enough.

Elijah had endured so much hardship. He cried out to God, "I've had enough. I want to die!" Elijah didn't understand what he really needed. He didn't need to die. He didn't even need to have God solve all his problems. He just needed God.

When you've had enough, God is enough.

EXPERIENCING GOD'S PRESENCE

So now back to my panic problem with content anxiety. So many messages to research and write and internalize. The pressure of coming up with creative ways of saying things and titling message series. A near-constant source of stress. I had an especially disquieting time struggling with this in 2019. ("Disquieting time" is a nice way of saying, "I had the biggest breakdown of my life.")

This was not a normal stretch of work and ministry for me. To be clear, it was my fault. I overscheduled, overstretched, and overworked. During that summer, I preached twenty-five messages in eight days in five cities in two countries.

Just before I ran that gauntlet, we discovered dangerous mold in five rooms of our house. While I was traveling internationally, those five rooms were being ripped out, and our home was under construction.

I also got word that a raccoon had gotten into our house, which is exactly what I needed. Every morning I had been praying, "God, if you could throw a raccoon into this nightmare month, that would be awesome."

And then, as if a raccoon weren't enough wildlife, a rat got into the car of an intern who was living with us, doing so much damage that his car wouldn't start.

Then my son's car wouldn't start.

That's about when the air conditioner in our house died. We were without air-conditioning for around ten days, right in the middle of summer in Oklahoma.

While my wife and I were traveling internationally, my credit card was compromised. It was the only card I let my kids use, so they couldn't buy anything.

When we returned to a mouse-infested construction zone under attack from a gang of wild raccoons, my oldest daughter gave birth to her first daughter. During the delivery, little baby McKenna went without oxygen for an extended period of time. After running tests, the doctors explained that our new granddaughter experienced significant brain damage. My family listened in dead silence as our hearts shattered into a million pieces.

Like Elijah, I had now had enough.

Miraculously, baby McKenna's story had a happy ending. She got better. While some think the doctors misdiagnosed her brain injuries, we think God heard our prayers and healed her. Either way, she is fine now. But I was not fine then. At all.

My world came crashing down, and my life came to a screeching halt.

On the back end of this season, my body shut down. It just stopped. Although I didn't go to the hospital, I did call a counselor. I knew I needed professional help.

Yes, I am a pastor, and yes, I am in counseling. I believe it is biblical and wise to get help from the wise. Sometimes we need to talk through our stuff with someone trained in talking through stuff. Someone who has no agenda except to help us get well.

I started meeting with a performance psychologist who helped me remember things I knew but had been ignoring. He helped me unpack my unusual, unhealthy, and unsustainable drive to produce and perform. He walked me through my decades of creating content.

I recognized how faithful God has always been in providing spiritual content for me to preach. I had a long track record of experience, and there was no reason to think he was going to stop now. Even more, my psychologist pointed me to the Lord. Staring at my stressors was obscuring my view of my savior.

Even if everything is entirely wrong, I still have a God who is entirely righteous. Even if I were left with nothing, I still have God, and he is everything.

I had to figure out how to stop being fixated on the presence of my problems and refocus on the presence of God. I had to once again lean in close to hear God's whisper.

I already knew what I discovered in counseling, but even still it felt like the surprise ending of an M. Night Shyamalan movie. But I had the aha moment I needed. I created a new declaration. Remember, in order for truth to set us free, we need to internalize it. It needs to live inside us so it becomes an automatic response. How do you replace an old rut with a new trench? Repetition.

The new, liberating declaration I tell myself again and again:

My experience plus God's presence is enough.

It's what Elijah learned. The experience he already had—with God providing miraculously for him, sustaining him through the worst of times—plus God's presence was enough.

The same is true for you. You might be feeling burdened, overwhelmed, and anxious. Maybe your soul feels crushed. What you need is the surprise ending you've known all along.

When you've had enough, God is enough.

Yes, the presence of problems is tempting you to panic. But don't ignore the presence of God. God is bigger than your problems.

" WHEN YOU'VE HAD ENOUGH, GOD IS ENOUGH. "

The most essential thing for your mind is for your mind to stay mindful about the presence of God.

Declare these next statements in your life, for your life. Say them out loud.

The Lord is close.

He is near.

He will never leave me nor forsake me.

Nothing can separate me from his love.

He is always with me. (He's with me right now as I
read this book.)

I am never alone, and he is enough for me.

His strength sustains me.

He watches over me, and he guides me with his
loving eye upon me.

God is close, and he wants to draw me close.

I will lean into him and listen for his whisper.

The LORD is righteous in all his ways
and faithful in all he does.
The LORD is near to all who call on him,
to all who call on him in truth.
He fulfills the desires of those who fear him;
he hears their cry and saves them.

—PSALM 145:17–19

--- EXERCISE 10 ---

WHEN YOU'VE HAD ENOUGH

What circumstances or dynamics exist in your life right now that regularly create panic for you?

Why do you think these specific situations create panic in you?

Is there any place in your life right now where you would say you have had enough and are at the end of your rope? Write it out.

What can you do to lean in and hear God's whisper among all the wind, fire, and earthquakes going on around you now in this circumstance?

Would talking to a counselor, pastor, or close friend help you get to a better place with this issue? If so, who?

GO BACK TO THE END OF THE CHAPTER AND READ OUT loud the declaration statements that I gave you. God is near. He is listening.

CHAPTER 11

THE PERSPECTIVE

OF PRAISE

WHY IS BEING MINDFUL OF GOD'S PRESENCE SO CRITICAL?

What I'm about to tell you may seem offensively simple, but it's indescribably important. Are you ready? Don't miss this.

If you forget God is there, you won't talk to him.

Simple, right? (I warned you.) But it's true. When we don't focus on God's presence, we don't pray. Instead we go it alone. We find our thoughts moving in the wrong direction, and our lives quickly follow.

But when we realize God is there, we realize we can talk to him. When things are bad, instead of just feeling down, we look up. We look up and find a God who loves us and has the power to help. We need to practice God's presence—habitually reminding ourselves that God is with us—so we'll be persistent in prayer.

Remember Paul's prescription in Philippians 4 for panic-inducing circumstances? "Do not be anxious about anything, but in every situation, by prayer and petition, with thanksgiving, present your requests to God" (v. 6).

Let this game-changing truth sink in:

- If it's big enough to worry about, then it's big enough to pray about.
- If it's on your mind, then it's on God's heart.

So pray.

If you are starting to experience some runaway negative thoughts—you're worried about your upcoming doctor's appointment, you don't know what decision to make, you are concerned about how your kid is doing in school, you feel like you are never going to find someone you want to marry—pray.

Something I've learned from years of being a pastor is that a lot of people aren't sure how to pray.

- Do I address God as my omnipotent Creator?
- Is praying in King James language mandatory?
- Do I have to sign off with the whole "In Jesus' name" part?
- Is the word harken required? I hope not, because I'm not sure I know what harken means.

The answer to these is a no.

In the garden of Gethsemane before his arrest, Jesus called

God *Abba*, the Aramaic word for father. *Abba* was the most simple, endearing way to refer to a father back then. Our equivalent might be *Daddy* or *Papa*. God is a relational God who loves you and wants to have an intimate relationship with you. You can call him Abba Father, the way Jesus did.

Paul wrote, "Present your requests to God," which may sound a little formal, but it's not. Another way of translating Paul's words is, "Let your needs be known." When you've had enough and your problems are tempting you to panic, how should you pray? Just let your needs be known.

I have six kids. I love them. I'm their abba, their daddy, Papa. My six kids have six different personalities, and they each let their needs be known in their own unique way.

My oldest daughter, Catie, lets her needs be known through texts. Her texts are loving but short, direct, and to the point.

My second oldest, Mandy, does not text; she calls. She's a talker. My average call with Mandy lasts about forty-three minutes. I've gone from being clean-shaven to having a sweet hipster beard in some of our epic conversations.

Anna makes formal presentations. She presents data and flip charts. I often feel unprepared and underdressed for our board-room conversations.

My son Sam waits until at least ten thirty at night. He shows up in our bedroom to talk, and his requests take a *long* time.

Stephen is our little attorney. He's smarter than anyone in the room. When he's asking, he's already got his defense prepared for any objections I might make. He's always three moves ahead of me.

My youngest, Joy, will ask, text, call, come into the room, sing, beg. She never surrenders and always gets what she wants, because she's the baby of the family. She is also everyone's favorite. Just ask her and she'll tell you.

Each of my kids is creative in how he or she asks, because they are not trying to do it "the right way"; they're just being themselves. God doesn't want you to do it "the right way" either. He wants you to be yourself, just like he made you. Let your needs be known in the way that feels right to you. Pray your way.

You might talk your prayers, yell your prayers, sing or journal them. You might pray long or you might pray short; just make sure you pray. There is no perfect way. Just pray.

When you pray, ask with confidence. I'm a dad, and I like it when my children need me. God is your perfect heavenly Father, and he loves it when you come to him and let your needs be known.

Peter told us that God invites us to go to him. "Humble yourselves, therefore, under God's mighty hand, that he may lift you up in due time. Cast all your anxiety on him because he cares for you" (1 Peter 5:6–7).

Do you feel down? Depleted? Like you've had enough? Do you feel like you're sinking? Peter said, "Humble yourselves . . . under God's mighty hand, that he may lift you up."

Those words will be more meaningful if you think about who wrote them. Peter is the one who was in the boat with the other disciples and had the audacity to believe he could get out and walk on water to Jesus. He was taking step after step on the Sea of Galilee, probably walking like a toddler at a trampoline park, when he noticed the wind and waves. His thoughts started to run, spiraling into negativity. He became fixated on the crashing waves and howling wind. The presence of problems caused him to ignore the presence of Jesus. So he sank.

Peter was drowning, so what did he do? He reached out to find Jesus' hand. Jesus lifted him up and saved him. Years later Peter had not forgotten, and he encouraged anyone who would read his letter, "Humble yourselves, therefore, under God's mighty hand, that he may lift you up."

THIS IS YOUR BRAIN ON PRAYER

Back to my 2019 summer crisis. With dozens of messages to write and meetings and traveling and the animal kingdom ambushing my home and every car in sight, I felt like I was drowning. I sought help from my counselor, and we came up with a strategy. The strategy was prayer. I decided to start tithing my study time in prayer.

I've always been a tither with my finances. I believe that God owns everything but trusts me with some of his money and asks me to give 10 percent back to him. I worship and honor him with the first 10 percent and trust him to bless the rest. Decades of tithing has taught me that 90 percent of what I have, with God's blessing, is way more than 100 percent without God's blessing.

I am now applying that principle to preaching. Instead of working harder, I'm praying harder. Instead of working longer, I'm praying longer. The strategy is based on my faith that if I give

90 percent of my work time to preparing and 10 percent to praying, I can get more done than I would if I worked for 100 percent of that time.

I believe that if I prepare my heart, God will help me prepare the message.

As I live out this strategy, I'm finding I am less anxious and have more assurance. Prayer has removed a lot of panic and replaced it with peace.

Prayer works. Prayer changes things. Perhaps more important, prayer changes *you*. Prayer changes your brain.

A few decades ago, neurologists believed the brain didn't change after adolescence. We know today that is not true. Our brains are constantly evolving. Neurologists call the process neuroplasticity. The idea is that we can sculpt our brain just as we can sculpt our muscles with some strategic time spent at the gym. Your brain is rewiring itself all the time by creating those new neural pathways. Each time you think a thought, it's easier to think that thought again. That's good news if you're thinking godly thoughts. It's not good news if you've been conditioned to run from blue vans.

> **" PRAYER WORKS. PRAYER CHANGES THINGS. PERHAPS MORE IMPORTANT, PRAYER CHANGES *YOU*. PRAYER CHANGES YOUR BRAIN. "**

Your brain is changing, and prayer changes your brain.

Dr. Andrew Newberg is the director of research at Thomas Jefferson Hospital and Medical College in Pennsylvania. He studies the brain by using neuroimaging techniques including functional magnetic resonance imaging, single-photon emission computed tomography, and positron emission tomography. I will shoot straight with you: I don't know what any of that means. But I do understand Dr. Newberg's conclusion. He writes, in scholarly articles and in books like *How God Changes Your Brain*, that prayer is like a physical workout for the brain and changes its chemistry.

Think about that. Not only does prayer touch the heart of God, but prayer changes the chemistry of your brain!

Another author in this field called neurotheology is Dr. Caroline Leaf, author of *Switch On Your Brain*. Her website says, "Dr. Caroline Leaf is a communication pathologist and cognitive neuroscientist with a Masters and PhD in Communication Pathology and a BSc in Logopaedics, specializing in cognitive and metacognitive neuropsychology."[7] I'm going to shoot straight with you again: I also don't know what any of that means!

Dr. Leaf writes, "It has been found that twelve minutes of daily focused prayer over an eight-week period can change the brain to such an extent that it can be measured on a brain scan. This type of prayer increases activity in brain areas associated with social interaction, compassion, and sensitivity to others. It also increases frontal lobe activity as focus and intentionality increase."[8]

Your life is always moving in the direction of your strongest thoughts. Worrying and toxic thinking will change your brain and move your life in a direction you don't want to go. Prayer changes your brain and moves your life in a positive direction.

Remember what Paul wrote? "Do not conform to the pattern of this world, but be transformed by the renewing of your mind" (Rom. 12:2).

From conforming to being transformed and renewed. Prayer literally renews our mind, leading us to God's peace and understanding. "And the peace of God, which transcends all understanding, will guard your hearts and your minds in Christ Jesus" (Phil. 4:7).

So why do we panic? It's that obnoxious amygdala. Scientists have a name for what happens to us, first coined by Daniel Goleman in his book *Emotional Intelligence*: an amygdala hijack. The amygdala gets a peek at what's going on out there and has an immediate, emotional, and overwhelming response, often a disproportionately excessive reaction. *Blue van! Run! Now!*

How do you avoid becoming a hostage to your amygdala? How do you counter its negative impact and not allow it to bully you into a panic?

You pray.

I know, I get it, that sounds like something pastors are supposed to say, but we can find peace through prayer! We can control our brains through prayer! It *is* something pastors say but also something scientists say. Another one of Dr. Andrew Newberg's findings startled the scientific community. He discovered that prayer can regulate and decrease the amygdala's fight-or-flight response.[9]

A scientist would call what happens to us when we panic, worry, and freak out an amygdala hijack. Paul, coming from a spiritual perspective, described this as sinful thinking. What is that?

Sinful thinking is not trusting the promises and power of God.

Prayer is choosing to trust the promises and power of God.

Prayer is deciding to turn to and surrender our feelings and control of our lives to God, trusting his promises and power. That's what we're going to do. We are going to pray in faith.

Paul wrote, "Those who are dominated by the sinful nature think about sinful things, but those who are controlled by the Holy Spirit think about things that please the Spirit. So letting your sinful nature control your mind leads to death. But letting the Spirit control your mind leads to life and peace" (Rom. 8:5–6 NLT).

If we let our natural, human nature take over, we will be led by runaway negative thoughts that spiral out of control and lead us in the wrong direction. If we let the Spirit take over, we will be led to life and peace.

This is why it is critical that we take every thought captive. With the power of the Holy Spirit, we are going to prayerfully employ the prefrontal cortex as a burly, thuggish bouncer standing outside the door of our minds, attentively checking IDs and not allowing in any thought that doesn't meet the criteria of being true, noble, right, lovely, admirable, excellent, or praiseworthy. If a thought is inconsistent with God's Word, we will wrestle it to the ground and make it obedient to Christ. If a thought sets itself up against the knowledge of God, we will demolish it with divine power, for we will not be dominated by dark thoughts that are self-destructive and displeasing to God.

THE GOD BOX

Through prayer and the power of God, we take every thought captive. Let me give you a visual way of thinking about this. I want you to actually do this.

Get a box. It doesn't have to be fancy or big: a small Amazon box or a shoebox. Now write, "God" on the box.

Every time you have a worry, burden, temptation, or runaway crazy thought, write it down on a slip of paper. You might write:

- I'm afraid I'm going to get fired.
- My seventeen-year-old son worries me sick.
- I want to get on my phone and go to websites or social media I know I shouldn't.
- I can't pay all these bills.
- What's going to happen with my mother?
- I want to smoke so bad.
- I'm never going to change.
- I'm angry with my spouse constantly.

Write them down and put them in your God box. When you do, pray, "God, I am trusting you with this. I know you are in control. I know you are bigger than this. This is not a thought I want to think, so I am giving this to you."

Once you pray and put the problem in the box, go on with your life.

From that point on, if you decide you want to worry about

whatever it was, go to the God box, take it out, and tell God, "I don't trust you with this. I am going to take it back from you."

When you read that last sentence, you probably thought, *I could never say that to God*, but every time we worry or panic, that *is* what we're saying to God.

That is not how we want to live, and we don't need to live that way. Paul told us, "The Lord is near," so we need to practice God's presence, so we'll be persistent in prayer. Peter told us we can cast all our cares on God, because he cares for us. Our thoughts seek to betray us, but we know:

- If it's big enough to worry about, it's big enough to pray about.
- If it's on your mind, it's on God's heart.

"Let us then approach God's throne of grace with confidence, so that we may receive mercy and find grace to help us in our time of need" (Heb. 4:16).

WHO, NOT WHAT

One particular week in the terrible, horrible, no good, very bad summer of 2019, I had a little less than two study days, with four full messages to write and preach.

There was the weekend message for our church, which is very important.

And there was our all-staff message, which is crucial because it's one of only four times a year when all of our church staff get together. These meetings drive the culture and spiritual passion of the church.

And a message to speak to one of my favorite ministries, Hope Is Alive, a great group of people overcoming addictions.

And a leadership podcast to do which, honestly, can reach as many people as everything else combined.

I was sitting at my desk, working on the message for our church. The topic was "The Perspective of Praise." It was not coming together. I started feeling even more anxious. I thought, *I can't get this one done. I've got three more to write. I can't do this. It's not going to work.* Suddenly I had trouble breathing. I realized I was letting negative thinking push me into a full-blown panic.

A thought hit me: *I'm writing a message telling the church to praise God. Maybe I should praise God.*

Then another thought: *But I don't want to. I want to get this message finished.*

Let's flash back a bit farther into the past. Paul is in prison. Not for a crime but for speaking about Jesus. He may be executed. He writes to his friends in Philippi, "Rejoice in the Lord always" (Phil. 4:4). Then he sounds like your mama because he repeats himself, just in case you aren't listening. "I will say it again: Rejoice!"

It's a great verse for a coffee mug with a pretty cursive font: "Rejoice in the Lord always!" It's perfect for a refrigerator magnet. Put it on a greeting card? Of course! It makes you sound spiritual if you tell your friends, "Rejoice in the Lord always!"

Full disclosure: I hate it when people quote that verse to me.

If I'm in the middle of a difficult situation, or I have a flat tire and it's 102 degrees out, or I just found out I need to have my tooth extracted, or my kid is sick. "Craig, you just need to rejoice in the Lord always!"

One reason I hate it is because I have to wonder about the person who says it. *Do you rejoice in the Lord always? Really?*

You might wonder about Paul. He told people to rejoice in the Lord when he was in prison! But did *he* rejoice in the Lord when he was in prison?

He did.

The jail cell in Rome from which Paul wrote to his friends in Philippi was not the first place he was in prison. Paul was often imprisoned for preaching Jesus. We read about one of those times in Acts 16. Interestingly, this time Paul was in jail in Philippi.

Paul was with his buddy Silas. I assume Paul called him Si. If your buddy ain't got a nickname, he ain't a buddy.

Paul and Silas healed a woman, which upset some people and led to a riot.

"The crowd joined in the attack against Paul and Silas, and the magistrates ordered them to be stripped and beaten with rods. After they had been severely flogged, they were thrown into prison, and the jailer was commanded to guard them carefully. When he received these orders, he put them in the inner cell and fastened their feet in the stocks. About midnight Paul and Silas were praying and singing hymns to God, and the other prisoners were listening to them" (Acts 16:22–25).

While likely you've never been stripped and beaten with rods, you may have been stripped of your confidence, your faith, or your dignity and beaten with doubts, anxiety, self-loathing. Perhaps you can relate to Paul and Silas a little.

Can you picture them? Thrown into prison, landing on the cold, hard ground with open wounds, maybe a broken nose, a couple of broken ribs. No doctor, nurse, bandaids, or ibuprofen.

Have you been there? Perhaps you hit the ground when you found out someone you love had cancer or that your kid was on drugs or that your spouse was cheating on you. In those tragic moments, what do you do?

What did Paul and Silas do?

They praised God.

What was Paul doing in prison? Rejoicing always.

I wonder how it happened?

Maybe Paul leaned over and said, "Hey, Si."

"Yeah?"

"Si, we're not dead."

"That's true, Paul."

"So I was just thinking. If we're not dead, we're not done."

"That's right!"

"You know what else, Si? Our God is still on the throne. Jesus is risen, still at the right hand of the Father. He's praying for us!"

"Yasss!"

"Si, I think we need to give him a little praise. Why don't we worship him?"

I don't know if that's how it went down, but there are three things I do know.

First, they were praising God for the who, not the what.

They were bloody and bound up in prison. If you had asked them, "What are you praising God for?" I don't think there was any what that they could point to. Nothing good was happening, but their God was still good. They weren't praising God for the what. They were praising him for the who. You can do that too.

> **"YOUR CIRCUMSTANCES MAY BE BAD, BUT YOUR GOD IS STILL GOOD."**

Your circumstances may be bad, but your God is still good. He is near, his promises are still true, his love still unconditional, his grace still amazing, his timing still perfect. You may not like the what of what's going on, but you can still praise God for the who of who he is.

Second, they were praising God before the provision.

So often we hold off on praising God until he provides what we want. Think about that. Doesn't it sound like an entitled little snot-nosed kid? *I won't be grateful until I get exactly what I want.* We are better than that and, more important, God deserves better. Paul and Silas praised God before he answered their prayers or changed their circumstances. That's the kind of person I want to be.

Third, they were praising God and *then* he showed up.

Paul and Silas were worshiping God in the middle of the night and—boom!—God showed up. "Suddenly, there was a massive earthquake, and the prison was shaken to its foundations. All the doors immediately flew open, and the chains of every prisoner fell off!" (Acts 16:26 NLT).

They did not praise God because he showed up; God showed up because they praised him.

I wonder if it's possible that you've been praying for God to show up for you in some way, thinking you'll be grateful and praise him when he does, while God is waiting for you to be grateful and praise him, and won't show up until you do.

So let's rejoice in the Lord always. Let's worship him now, no matter our what, for who he is. Let's praise him and—spoiler alert—God will show up. He will shake your cell, chains will fall off, and doors will swing open.

Paul wrote, "Rejoice in the Lord always" to his friends in Philippi from his prison cell in Rome, because he had been in prison cells before, including in Philippi. He knew what happens when we praise God even before he provides. God shows up. God shows off.

That's what happened to me. Remember, I was sitting at my desk with four messages to write. The one I was working on, "The Perspective of Praise," was not coming together. Panic was setting in. A thought hit me: *I'm writing a message telling the church to praise God. Maybe I should praise God.* Then another thought: *I don't want to.*

Just then my amygdala and my prefrontal cortex started debating.

But Craig, you're going to tell them to praise God. Doesn't it make sense for you to do it?

You know what, Groeschel, we don't need your opinion.

C'mon, Craig. Spend some time worshiping. That's what you're going to tell them to do. You do it.

Listen, Groeschel, I will tell them. I'm the pastor; that's my job. They'll listen to me. But I don't want to.

Dude, really?

Okay, fine!

I started trying to praise God. Honestly, there wasn't much faith in it. It wasn't deep praise. It was more like, *Alright, God. Well, I'm pretty convinced you're still there. I guess. But I do have all these messages to write. You could help me. It'd be nice. Anyway, I know you're there. And I think you are gonna do something. I mean, you've done a lot for me before. Actually, I have been in this position before, and you have always come through for me. You really are a good God. All the time. God, you are good. God, I do trust you. God, you always provide for me. I love you, God. I'm so thankful, God.*

Then I started crying.

My spirit began to break, and my work ethic took a back seat. My initial petulance turned into intense praise. I realized I was having a full-blown worship service. Right there at my desk. Just me and God.

He showed up in the middle of my praising him. I confess my praise began pretty half-hearted, but God is always gracious and he showed up anyway.

It's time for us to fix our thoughts on God, to give him praise for who he is, regardless of what he may or may not be doing.

When we praise him, he will show up.

When he shows up, it will change our thinking.

If we change our thoughts, we change our life.

Guess what? Even more will change. When we praise God, it also changes our perspective and our brain. And that's where we're going next.

--- EXERCISE 11 ---

YOUR GOD BOX

THE EXERCISE FOR THIS CHAPTER IS SIMPLY TO DO EXACTLY what I recommended in the section called "The God Box."

Get a box, write down your problems, pray about them, and put them inside. I get that doing this may feel a little strange at first, but there is just something about the symbolism and the action of placing your problems in the box, giving them to God. And then, if you choose to worry, having to take them back out and confess your struggle to him. What if this simple exercise changes your prayer life and what God does in your life? That would be worth any effort, right?

CHAPTER 12

LOOK THROUGH, NOT AT

I HAVE A CONFESSION TO MAKE. WELL, ACTUALLY TWO.

First, I thought you were lying. Actually, I thought every single person on planet Earth was lying. Lying about what, you ask? Magic Eye.

Magic Eye is the picture with little dots all over it that looks like nothing but a mix of colors. Yet some people, many people, claim that if you look at it in the right way, then a 3D image will pop out. Suddenly you're seeing a circus or horses or an eagle soaring through the sky. Well, I could never see the magic 3D image. I thought everyone was lying.

But my second and real confession: I think I am Magic Eye challenged. I accepted my inability as a cross I would have to bear, until one day when the stars aligned on a family vacation. We visited a wax museum. (I am not proud of that.) Amid all the wax statues was a—yep—Magic Eye picture.

I decided I had come to the museum for such a time as this.

I was not going to leave until I saw something 3D. I would die in that stupid museum if I had to. I needed a Magic Eye guide to lead me into the promised land, so I asked a teenager who worked there to help me.

He began to instruct me in a Bill-and-Ted kind of way. "Bro, you just have to kinda like, well, squat down, like, ya know, you're about to catch a ground ball."

I played ball, so I got down into ready position.

He told me, "Okay, bro. Now don't look at it. Look *through* it."

I was confused. How do you look through it?

Somewhat impatiently, he encouraged me. "You know, look through it. Like, not at it. Like, beyond it. Look beyond. Look through."

I looked through it. I kept looking through it. I looked through it so long, I think I finally got drunk. I'm not sure if you can technically get drunk looking through a Magic Eye picture, but that's what happened to me. I was squatting, ready to catch a ground ball, looking not at but through, like, beyond, when it happened! Three-dimensional dolphins jumped off the picture! I was so excited, I threw up my hands in victory. *I once was lost but now am found. Was blind but now I see—3D dolphins!*

When I threw my hands into the air, I lost it. I lost the dolphins. I never saw them again. But there is no denying that what happened between us was real. I felt it. The dolphins felt it. My bro guide felt it. We may never meet again, but we'll always have that wax museum.

If you are Magic Eye impaired like me but want to have a

dreamy rendezvous with some friendly sea creatures, let me be your guide: look through or beyond; there is no look at.

Developing magic eyes is all about perspective.

When we practice God's presence—always mindful that he is near—we will pray, and when we pray, that leads us to praise.

Praising God is all about perspective. A change of perspective leads us to praise God, and praising God changes our perspective.

> **❝ PRAISING GOD IS ALL ABOUT PERSPECTIVE. ❞**

The fourth tool I've learned that has powerfully impacted my thinking and my life is the Rejoice Principle: Revive your soul, reclaim your life. I stay mindful of God's presence; I praise him.

When I've had enough, I pray, putting my concerns in my God box.

I praise God—for the who, not the what—even when I don't want to.

And I sense my perspective changing.

LOOK AT WHAT'S RIGHT

Paul wanted to be in Rome, but not in a prison cell. He wanted to preach, not be a prisoner. Nothing was going the way he'd hoped.

From that jail, in chains, Paul wrote his letter to the Philippians. Remember when we saw in part 3 how Paul reframed what he was going through? Instead of complaining that he couldn't preach to the government officials like he wanted, he praised God for the opportunity he'd been given to preach to the prison guards. He didn't feel thwarted; he was thrilled. He wrote, "Because of this I rejoice." Then he added, "Yes, and I will continue to rejoice, for I know that through your prayers and God's provision of the Spirit of Jesus Christ what has happened to me will turn out for my deliverance. I eagerly expect and hope that I will in no way be ashamed, but will have sufficient courage so that now as always Christ will be exalted in my body, whether by life or by death. For to me, to live is Christ and to die is gain" (Phil. 1:18–21).

While everything seemed negative, Paul chose to see the positive. Paul was looking not at it but through it. He was seeing the image God wanted him to see that others couldn't. That's why, as he continued the letter, he wrote, "The Lord is near" (Phil. 4:5) and, "Do not be anxious about anything" (v. 6) and, "The peace of God, which transcends all understanding, will guard your hearts and your minds in Christ Jesus" (v. 7). It's why he could tell his readers, "Rejoice in the Lord always" (v. 4).

How could he praise God in jail? Perspective. It's not about prison but about perspective.

When we look through our circumstances with perspective, we know there is always reason to praise God.

Remember when I got back from my hellacious trip and decided to start seeing a counselor? At one appointment he asked me, "How bad is it?"

I told him, "I'm in trouble."

We went through a long series of questions. At the end my counselor said, "Well, I've got really good news for you. You're not in that much trouble."

I said, "No, you don't understand. I *am* in trouble."

He smiled. "No, you don't understand. You're not in that much trouble. I mean, I know trouble, and you're not in that much trouble. You have an issue that is very real, but when you look at everything else, you've got so much good in your life."

Because I was in panic mode, I looked at him suspiciously.

He said, "Physically, you're in really great shape. Your diet is almost flawless. You're not abusing any kind of substances. You're ridiculously in love with your wife. You have a great relationship with your kids. You're not missing family events. You've got incredible relationships around you, a lot of people who really care about you."

I nodded. Because he was right.

The counselor continued. "There are so many things that are right. The reason you're panicking is because you're just looking at what's wrong. Don't forget to also look at what's right."

He nailed it. I was looking at, not through. I was staring at my problems, having lost perspective on all the ways God had blessed my life. I left the counselor's office praising God.

I don't know what problems you're staring at right now. You might have a big one and a complicated one and an annoying one. I'm not minimizing your issues. I know they are real. But don't forget to look through. Look at the whole picture. Do you have family? Friends? A church? Your health? A home? Some food in the fridge? Some money in the bank? Your faith?

Don't just look at what's wrong. Look at what's right. Maybe take a minute to write down all the good things. Literally count your blessings and thank God for them.

A change of perspective leads us to praise God.

And praising God changes our perspective.

We often see this in the Psalms. The psalmist might begin by recounting what's wrong in his life: enemies are attacking; he is feeling rejected by God; he's been falsely accused; he has spotty cell

> ❝ A CHANGE OF PERSPECTIVE LEADS US TO PRAISE GOD. AND PRAISING GOD CHANGES OUR PERSPECTIVE. ❞

phone coverage. Then he commands himself to praise God anyway. Here are some examples:

- "Why, my soul, are you downcast? Why so disturbed within me? Put your hope in God, for I will yet praise him, my Savior and my God" (Ps. 42:5).
- "Bless the LORD, O my soul; and all that is within me, bless His holy name! Bless the LORD, O my soul, and forget not all His benefits" (Ps. 103:1–2 NKJV).
- "Praise the LORD! Praise the LORD, O my soul! While I live I will praise the LORD; I will sing praises to my God while I have my being" (Ps. 146:1–2 NKJV).

The psalmist is reading from the Bad Perspective Version but forces himself to praise God, and then—bam!—a changed perspective:

- "By day the LORD directs his love, at night his song is with me—a prayer to the God of my life" (Ps. 42:8).

- "The LORD has established his throne in heaven, and his kingdom rules over all. Praise the LORD, you his angels, you mighty ones who do his bidding, who obey his word. Praise the LORD, all his heavenly hosts, you his servants who do his will. Praise the LORD, all his works everywhere in his dominion. Praise the LORD, my soul" (Ps. 103:19–22).

That's what happened to me at my desk that day. I was in the midst of panic, but I forced myself to praise, and praising God changed my perspective. I went from looking at my problems and seeing overwhelming obstacles to looking through my problems and seeing an omnipotent God who was right there with me.

Praising God changes our perspective.

And praising God changes our brains.

That's been verified too.

Praise, like prayer, affects the amygdala, diminishing the fight-or-flight mechanism.[10] Worshiping God has even been shown to decrease heart rate, blood pressure, blood glucose levels, and serum markers of inflammation.[11]

That's not all.

Remember Dr. Newberg, the brain scientist? He has proven that praising and worshiping God leads to quantifiable changes in brain volume and metabolism, especially in a part of the brain called the cingulate cortex. Turns out, an increase in the volume of the cingulate cortex results in increased capacity for compassionate thinking and feeling.[12] So, basically, the more the cingulate grows, the more empathetic you become.

That's what happened to me. That day at my desk, when I was stuck while writing my message, I made myself praise God. Praising him changed my perspective and gave me my message. Moments earlier I could not come up with a message, but then I felt overwhelmed by it.

I was writing a message about having a perspective of praise, even in the midst of anxiety. I realized I had not struggled much with anxiety or with not feeling like praising God. In the past, I could not have had deep empathy for the people I'd be speaking to, because I had never really felt it. But my miserable summer of angst had put me in that place, and I had to learn how to fix my thoughts and fight out of it. That's when it hit me. With a bad perspective, *I've had enough* and *I can't handle this*, but through a perspective of praise, *I want you to know, brothers and sisters, that what has happened to me has served to advance the gospel.*

I felt more compassion for struggling people. I don't know if it was because I was pumping up my cingulate cortex, but I knew I couldn't wait to share this message with hurting people.

Praise changed my perspective.

I knew it would change theirs.

And I know it will change yours.

DON'T DROP YOUR GUARD

I am no good with Magic Eye, but I've got serious nunchuck skills. For real! I am legitimately good with nunchucks. I have taken classes in several martial arts: aikido, tae kwon do, and jiujitsu.

Also, I have watched *Karate Kid* probably thirty times, and I can do Mr. Miyagi's crane kick with the best of them.

My best training came from working with a childhood friend named Jody Nolan. Jody, who has black belts in several martial arts, became a professional stuntman and a sparring partner for Chuck Norris.

Back when we were in eleventh grade, we put on full pads and headgear. We were going at it. I felt like I was holding my own. I thought, *I really am pretty dang good.* That's when Jody asked, "Are you ready to go hard?" *Umm, I thought we were already going hard.* I knew I couldn't back down, so I looked at Jody and said, "Bring it." Jody brought it. The problem was that when I said, "Bring it," I think I was a little afraid, and I lowered my guard for a second. It went down like this:

Jody: "Are you ready to go hard?"

Me: "Bring it."

Jody: Sends something—I think maybe a cinder block—crashing into my face. (I found out later Jody hit me with a spinning backfist that I never saw coming.)

Me: Suddenly lying on my back, with little cartoon stars and birds spinning around my head.

Jody: "You dropped your guard! I told you, never drop your guard. Whatever you do, don't drop your guard!"

As we near the end of our journey, I hope you walk away

understanding that your thinking determines so much. Your life always moves in the direction of your strongest thoughts. What consumes your mind controls your life.

I also hope you remember that, unfortunately, your mind is under attack.

Just after encouraging us to humble ourselves and cast all our anxiety on God, Peter wrote, "Be alert and of sober mind. Your enemy the devil prowls around like a roaring lion looking for someone to devour" (1 Peter 5:8).

Peter said, "Be alert." Don't drop your guard! Why? You have an enemy, the devil, and he is looking for someone to devour. The devil is always coming after you, he is always swinging, and so you always have to keep your hands up.

How do we do that?

Remember what Paul wrote: "Do not be anxious about anything, but in every situation, by prayer and petition, with thanksgiving, present your requests to God. And the peace of God, which transcends all understanding, will guard your hearts and your minds in Christ Jesus" (Phil. 4:6–7).

Paul calls for us to make petitions and offer thanksgiving. Or we could say, prayer and praise. The promise is, if we do that, God will guard our minds. His peace will guard our minds.

Peace guards your heart and your mind.

Peace is preceded by prayer and praise.

In a fight, you need to keep both hands up to protect yourself. Think of prayer as one hand and praise as the other. We need to keep both hands raised.

When someone raises both hands, that can be to surrender or to celebrate a victory. When we raise both hands to God, it is both—surrendering to God and fully anticipating the victory that is already ours, because we know we are more than conquerors though him who loves us.

The devil's target is your mind. His weapon is his lies. He will never stop trying to deceive you. There are lies he's been telling you your entire life. Right now he's seeking out opportunities to tell you new lies. He is probably taking a swing at you as you read this, and he will again in the next few minutes, hours, days, and weeks.

What do we do?

We keep our guard up.

We go to God with prayer, and we go to God with praise.

Surrender *and* victory.

— EXERCISE 12 —

EVALUATING WHAT'S RIGHT

What circumstance or relationship in your life right now do you need to stop looking at and instead look through to see what God is doing?

In what circumstance or relationship in your life right now do you need to look at what's right instead of seeing only what's wrong?

In what circumstance or relationship in your life right now have you dropped your guard and know you need to raise both hands to God, both surrendering to him and fully anticipating the victory?

CHOOSING TO

WIN THE WAR

BECAUSE, LIKE YOU, EVERY DAY I FEEL LIKE I HAVE MORE than I can handle, I rely on God to renew my mind. His truth is my battle plan. I continue to create new trenches of truth to replace my old ruts so they will give me thought pathways leading to life and peace.

When I feel distracted by the things of this world and driven to please people instead of serve God, I will remind myself:

> Jesus is first in my life.
> I exist to serve and glorify him.

When I start to slide toward selfishness and take my wife and kids for granted, I will declare by faith:

I love my wife, and I will lay down my life to serve her.
I will raise my children to love God and serve him
with their whole hearts.
I will nurture, equip, train, and empower them to do
more for the kingdom than they ever thought
possible.

When I have a negative attitude about people and find myself criticizing others more than loving them, I will write it, say it, and repeat it until I believe it:

I love people. And believe the best about others.

When I feel lazy, apathetic, and spiritually lethargic, I will remind myself of the truth:

I am disciplined.
Christ in me is stronger than the wrong desires in me.

When the devil tries to tempt me to be self-absorbed, self-obsessed, or self-destructive, I will say by faith:

I am growing closer to Jesus every day.
Because of Christ, my family is closer, my body is
stronger, my faith is deeper, my leadership is
sharper.

When I feel overwhelmed in my calling and doubt my ability to lead, I will choose to believe that:

I am creative, innovative, driven, focused, and
blessed beyond measure because the spirit of
God dwells within me.

When I fall back into my old negative mindsets, worrying or obsessing about money, I will remember:

Money is not and never will be a problem for me.
My God is an abundant provider who meets every need.
Because I am blessed, I will always be a blessing.
I will lead the way with irrational generosity, because I
know it's truly more blessed to give than to receive.

When I don't feel adequate to help others succeed, I will remind myself that:

I develop leaders. That's not something I do; it's
who I am.

When I'm feeling sorry for myself because my calling is hard or the critics are loud, I will remember:

Pain is my friend.
I rejoice in suffering, because Jesus suffered for me.

When I start to think that what I do doesn't matter, that I'm not making a difference, I will counter that lie with the truth:

I bring my best and then some.
It's what I bring after I bring my best that makes the difference.
The world will be different and better because I served Jesus today.

Where do *you* need Jesus today, right now?
Where are your thoughts falling short of his life-giving truth?
Are you stuck in a negative, hurtful, and poisonous rut?
What will you do?
You will use the four tools God has given us to fix our thoughts and win the war in our minds: (1) the Replacement Principle, (2) the Rewire Principle, (3) the Reframe Principle, and (4) the Rejoice Principle.

1. *You will remove the lie and replace it with truth.* We know we have an enemy who is seeking to destroy us. His weapon is the lie. Our weakness is believing lies, and if we believe a lie, it will affect our lives as if it were true.

The problem is that we don't realize that the lies we believe are lies. If we knew, we wouldn't believe them. Hopefully, the lies you need to defeat are now clear to you.

2. *You will create new trenches of truth.* Our brains have neural pathways—mental ruts we created through repeatedly thinking the same thoughts—which trigger our automatic response to

external stimuli. To stop a behavior, we need to remove the lie behind it and replace the neural pathway. We dig truth trenches.

How?

You renew your mind with God's truth. As you internalize Bible verses, they will become your new way of thinking and responding.

You will form personal declarations, writing them, thinking them, and confessing them until you believe them. These declarations of God's truth about you will become your new mental pathways to life and peace.

3. *You will reframe and preframe.* We cannot control what happens to us, but we can control how we perceive it. We all have cognitive biases that cause us to see things in ways that do not reflect reality. But we have the power to do cognitive reframing, changing how we view the past and the future.

4. *You will change your perspective through prayer and praise.* It's easy to feel overwhelmed by everything that is happening, but when we've had enough, God is enough.

Not only is God enough; God is near. We stay mindful of his presence. When we do, it leads us to pray. Instead of worrying, we put all our fears in our God box, trusting his love and provision for us. Praying changes our brain, as does praising God. We praise him for the who of who he is, even if the what is not what we want. As we praise God, he shows up and gives us peace of mind.

Decide today that you will not think like the rest of the world. You will let God renew your mind.

Instead of becoming fixated on what you see, fix your thoughts on Jesus. He made you. He will sustain you. He can carry you, strengthen you, and empower you to do what he's called you to do.

So don't drop your guard! Take captive every lie your enemy whispers in your ear. You know you are not someone who needs something other than God, because you know God is everything.

You are not controlled by fear.

You are not stuck.

You are not a slave to your habits.

You are not a prisoner to your addictions.

You are not a victim.

You are not failing.

You are not unlikable.

You are not unworthy of love.

You are not your past.

You are not what you did.

You are not what someone else did to you.

You are not who others say you are.

You are not who your unhealthy thoughts say you are.

You are not done.

You. Are. Who. God. Says. You. Are.

Because of Christ:

You are loved.

You are forgiven.

You are healed.

You are new.

You are redeemed.

You are free.

You are blessed.

You are strong and mighty.

You are chosen.

You are empowered.

You are a weapon of righteousness in a world of darkness.

Let the truth about you trickle in, become a torrent, and transform you.

Your God is with you. He will never leave you nor forsake you.

Your God is for you. He will fight for you. No weapon formed against you will prosper. You are more than a conqueror through him.

Your God is enough for you. He is more than enough.

Nothing can separate you from God's love. Not death. Not demons. Not the present nor the past. Nothing will ever separate you from the love of God that is in Christ Jesus our Lord.

Let God change your thinking.

He will change your life.

AFTERWORD

By Amy Groeschel

MY HUSBAND, CRAIG, IS MY BEST FRIEND AND ONE OF THE godliest people I've ever known. His life is characterized by good spiritual fruit, but he's not perfect. His life, like everyone else's, is a work in progress. And this book is a reflection of more hard work than I can describe. When I say hard work, I'm not just referring to the hours of research, writing, and rewriting. I'm talking about the hard work of renewing his mind from chronic negativity to believing and living out God's truth.

When people brag on my husband, they talk about his passion, his servant leadership, his gift of clearly communicating the gospel, and his self-discipline. I've been married to him for thirty years, and I can tell you firsthand, he really is a man pursuing God's heart and glory. But what people may not see is that Craig's admirable qualities are testimonies of an overcoming faith that has endured years of waging war against discouraging thoughts in his mind.

Like many people, Craig has always been hard on himself. Whether competing in a sport, preaching a sermon, or leading our family, he often was disappointed he didn't do better. When people looked on and admired him, internally he was wrestling with thoughts like "I can never measure up" or "I don't have what it takes."

His negative thoughts weren't limited to personal critique. Craig often worried and obsessed about things to come. Rather than thinking thoughts of faith, his mind seemed to drift toward worry and anxiety.

As a wife who adores her husband, I did my best to encourage, speak life over him, and pray for him. Slowly but surely, Craig recognized he was losing a war in his mind. Once he recognized it for what it was—a spiritual battle—Craig's attitude toward it changed. If there is one thing I can promise you about my husband, it's that he refuses to lose a battle.

When he realized he was allowing our spiritual enemy to sidetrack his faith, Craig fought back with a spiritual vengeance. It started with a study of any Bible verse that mentions thoughts, the mind, or thinking. Craig memorized and internalized them. Then he began learning how God created our minds to function. When he discovered that our brains create neural pathways that make it easier to keep thinking the same thoughts, he became more determined and more encouraged that he could win this battle in his mind.

Second Corinthians 10:3–5 became his strongest weapon in the battle. Paul writes, "For though we live in the world, we do not wage war as the world does. The weapons we fight with are not the weapons of the world. On the contrary, they have divine power to demolish strongholds. We demolish arguments and every pretension that sets itself up against the knowledge of God, and we take captive every thought to make it obedient to Christ."

That is exactly what Craig did. He started to name and write down any thought that is inconsistent with God's truth. He captured all the wrong thoughts, discouraging voices, and hurtful lies that echoed in his mind.

Then, one by one, Craig found Bible verses that corrected the harmful thoughts with encouraging spiritual truths.

That's when the positive changes started happening.

Before long, Craig had created a list of positive, faith-filled spiritual declarations designed to renew his mind with truth. By meditating on truth, Craig deprogrammed his negative and fearful thinking. His mind was being renewed and his faith was strengthening. I saw his attitude and communication change.

Craig is now filled with God's peace and hope. His mind is grounded in the Word of God. His confidence is firmly placed in Christ and not in his gifts, talents, or strengths.

It's obvious to me that God is doing a beautiful work of perfecting Craig—and me. Since you've been reading this book, I'm guessing he is working in you too. I'm so grateful God doesn't leave us stuck where we are but is committed to our becoming like Christ.

Sometimes people wonder whether our marriage is really as strong as it looks. I will tell you humbly, and with much gratitude, it is. But good, strong relationships don't come without a lot of effort. In marriage, we get to see each other's struggles up close, and we have the wonderful opportunity to serve our spouses daily with grace, prayers, and life-giving encouragement. Craig had a war going on in his mind. With Christ's help, he is winning that war. He did the work of changing his thinking, and God has changed his life.

I'm thankful to have this opportunity to communicate how much I love him, and always will, and how very proud I am of his full devotion to our savior, Jesus.

And I want to encourage you: Don't be discouraged. With Jesus, you can win the war in your mind. You *can* change your thinking, and God can change your life.

BIBLE VERSES FOR
WINNING THE WAR

USE THESE PASSAGES IN THE EXERCISES AT THE END OF
each chapter. Better yet, memorize them and think on them daily.
Allow the words of God to renew your mind.

- Scripture quotations are listed in the order they appear in
  the book.
- When any Scripture reference is made in the book, the
  entire verse or passage is included here.
- Some verses are repeated in each of the four parts.

INTRODUCTION

Finally, brothers and sisters, whatever is true, whatever
is noble, whatever is right, whatever is pure, whatever is
lovely, whatever is admirable—if anything is excellent or
praiseworthy—think about such things. Whatever you have
learned or received or heard from me, or seen in me—put it
into practice. And the God of peace will be with you.

—PHILIPPIANS 4:8–9

As he thinks in his heart, so is he.

—PROVERBS 23:7 NKJV

PART 1: THE REPLACEMENT PRINCIPLE

Remove the Lies, Replace with Truth

God has not given us a spirit of fear, but of power and of love and of a sound mind.

—2 TIMOTHY 1:7 NKJV

We are not fighting against flesh-and-blood enemies, but against evil rulers and authorities of the unseen world, against mighty powers in this dark world, and against evil spirits in the heavenly places.

—EPHESIANS 6:12 NLT

"The thief comes only to steal and kill and destroy; I have come that they may have life, and have it to the full."

—JOHN 10:10

We wanted to come to you—certainly I, Paul, did, again and again—but Satan blocked our way.

—1 THESSALONIANS 2:18

Be alert and of sober mind. Your enemy the devil prowls around like a roaring lion looking for someone to devour.

—1 PETER 5:8

"You belong to your father, the devil, and you want to carry out your father's desires. He was a murderer from the beginning, not holding to the truth, for there is no truth in him. When he lies, he speaks his native language, for he is a liar and the father of lies."

—JOHN 8:44

I do not understand what I do. For what I want to do I do not do, but what I hate I do. And if I do what I do not want to do, I agree that the law is good. As it is, it is no longer I myself who do it, but it is sin living in me. For I know that good itself does not dwell in me, that is, in my sinful nature. For I have the desire to do what is good, but I cannot carry it out. For I do not do the good I want to do, but the evil I do not want to do—this I keep on doing. Now if I do what I do not want to do, it is no longer I who do it, but it is sin living in me that does it.

So I find this law at work: Although I want to do good, evil is right there with me. For in my inner being I delight in God's law; but I see another law at work in me, waging war against the law of my mind and making me a prisoner of the law of sin at work within me. What a wretched man I am! Who will rescue me from this body that is subject to death?

—ROMANS 7:15–24

I know what it is to be in need, and I know what it is to have plenty. I have learned the secret of being content in any and every situation, whether well fed or hungry, whether living in plenty or in want.

—PHILIPPIANS 4:12

Though we live in the world, we do not wage war as the world does. The weapons we fight with are not the weapons of the world. On the contrary, they have divine power to demolish strongholds. We demolish arguments and every pretension that sets itself up against the knowledge of God, and we take captive every thought to make it obedient to Christ.

—2 CORINTHIANS 10:3–5

One who is wise can go up against the city of the mighty and pull down the stronghold in which they trust.

—PROVERBS 21:22

I also pray that you will understand the incredible greatness of God's power for us who believe him. This is the same mighty power that raised Christ from the dead and seated him in the place of honor at God's right hand in the heavenly realms.

—EPHESIANS 1:19–20 NLT

Now the serpent was more crafty than any of the wild animals the LORD God had made. He said to the woman, "Did God really say, 'You must not eat from any tree in the garden'?"

The woman said to the serpent, "We may eat fruit from the trees in the garden, but God did say, 'You must not eat fruit from the tree that is in the middle of the garden, and you must not touch it, or you will die.'"

"You will not certainly die," the serpent said to the woman. "For God knows that when you eat from it your eyes will be opened, and you will be like God, knowing good and evil."

—GENESIS 3:1–5

I am afraid that just as Eve was deceived by the serpent's cunning, your minds may somehow be led astray from your sincere and pure devotion to Christ.

—2 CORINTHIANS 11:3

The heart is deceitful above all things
    and beyond cure.
    Who can understand it?

—JEREMIAH 17:9

There is a way that appears to be right,
    but in the end it leads to death.

—PROVERBS 14:12

The word of God is alive and active. Sharper than any double-edged sword, it penetrates even to dividing soul and spirit, joints and marrow; it judges the thoughts and attitudes of the heart.

—HEBREWS 4:12

Take the helmet of salvation and the sword of the Spirit, which is the word of God.

—EPHESIANS 6:17

Do not conform to the pattern of this world, but be transformed by the renewing of your mind. Then you will be able to test and approve what God's will is—his good, pleasing and perfect will.

—ROMANS 12:2

Opponents must be gently instructed, in the hope that God will grant them repentance leading them to a knowledge of the truth, and that they will come to their senses and escape from the trap of the devil, who has taken them captive to do his will.

—2 TIMOTHY 2:25–26

"Then you will know the truth, and the truth will set you free."

—JOHN 8:32

Jesus was led by the Spirit into the wilderness to be tempted by the devil. After fasting forty days and forty nights, he was hungry. The tempter came to him and said, "If you are the Son of God, tell these stones to become bread."

Jesus answered, "It is written: 'Man shall not live on bread alone, but on every word that comes from the mouth of God.'"

—MATTHEW 4:1–4 (REF. DEUT. 8:3)

Then the devil took him to the holy city and had him stand on the highest point of the temple. "If you are the

Son of God," he said, "throw yourself down. For it is
written:

> "'He will command his angels concerning you,
>
> and they will lift you up in their hands,
>
> so that you will not strike your foot against a stone.'"

—MATTHEW 4:5–6 (REF. PS. 91:11–12)

Jesus answered him, "It is also written: 'Do not put the
Lord your God to the test.'"

—MATTHEW 4:7 (REF. DEUT. 6:16)

Again, the devil took him to a very high mountain and
showed him all the kingdoms of the world and their
splendor. "All this I will give you," he said, "if you will
bow down and worship me."

Jesus said to him, "Away from me, Satan! For it is
written: 'Worship the Lord your God, and serve him
only.'"

—MATTHEW 4:8–10 (REF. DEUT. 6:13)

Then the devil left him, and angels came and
attended him.

—MATTHEW 4:11

I can do all this through him who gives me strength.

—PHILIPPIANS 4:13

Rejoice in the Lord always. I will say it again: Rejoice!

—PHILIPPIANS 4:4

"Come to me, all you who are weary and burdened, and I will give you rest. Take my yoke upon you and learn from me, for I am gentle and humble in heart, and you will find rest for your souls. For my yoke is easy and my burden is light."

—MATTHEW 11:28–30

Cast all your anxiety on him because he cares for you.

—1 PETER 5:7

God is our refuge and strength,
an ever-present help in trouble.

—PSALM 46:1

What, then, shall we say in response to these things? If God is for us, who can be against us?

—ROMANS 8:31

In all these things we are more than conquerors through him who loved us.

—ROMANS 8:37

God demonstrates his own love for us in this: While we were still sinners, Christ died for us.

—ROMANS 5:8

He who did not spare his own Son, but gave him up for us all—how will he not also, along with him, graciously give us all things?

—ROMANS 8:32

You created my inmost being;

> you knit me together in my mother's womb.

I praise you because I am fearfully and

> wonderfully made;
>
> your works are wonderful,
>
> I know that full well.

My frame was not hidden from you

> when I was made in the secret place,
>
> when I was woven together in the depths of the earth.

Your eyes saw my unformed body;

> all the days ordained for me were written in your
>
> book
>
> before one of them came to be.

—PSALM 139:13–16

You know that it was not with perishable things such as silver or gold that you were redeemed from the empty way of life handed down to you from your ancestors, but with the precious blood of Christ, a lamb without blemish or defect.

—1 PETER 1:18–19

PART 2: THE REWIRE PRINCIPLE

Rewire Your Brain, Renew Your Mind

Do not conform to the pattern of this world, but be transformed by the renewing of your mind. Then you will be able to test and approve what God's will is—his good, pleasing and perfect will.

—ROMANS 12:2

I have hidden your word in my heart
that I might not sin against you.

—PSALM 119:11

I know what it is to be in need, and I know what it is to have plenty. I have learned the secret of being content in any and every situation, whether well fed or hungry, whether living in plenty or in want.

—PHILIPPIANS 4:12

"Just as you, Judah and Israel, have been a curse among the nations, so I will save you, and you will be a blessing. Do not be afraid, but let your hands be strong."

—ZECHARIAH 8:13

"In everything I did, I showed you that by this kind of hard work we must help the weak, remembering the words the Lord Jesus himself said: 'It is more blessed to give than to receive.'"

—ACTS 20:35

God is able to bless you abundantly, so that in all things at all times, having all that you need, you will abound in every good work.

—2 CORINTHIANS 9:8

God will meet all your needs according to the riches of
his glory in Christ Jesus.

—PHILIPPIANS 4:19

For God bought you with a high price. So you must
honor God with your body.

—1 CORINTHIANS 6:20 NLT

Jesus replied, "I am the bread of life. Whoever comes to
me will never be hungry again. Whoever believes in me
will never be thirsty."

—JOHN 6:35 NLT

> LORD, my strength and my fortress,
>   my refuge in time of distress,
> to you the nations will come
>   from the ends of the earth and say,
> "Our ancestors possessed nothing but false gods,
>   worthless idols that did them no good."

—JEREMIAH 16:19

What, then, shall we say in response to these things? If
God is for us, who can be against us? He who did not
spare his own Son, but gave him up for us all—how
will he not also, along with him, graciously give us all
things? Who will bring any charge against those whom
God has chosen? It is God who justifies. Who then
is the one who condemns? No one. Christ Jesus who
died—more than that, who was raised to life—is at the

right hand of God and is also interceding for us. Who shall separate us from the love of Christ? Shall trouble or hardship or persecution or famine or nakedness or danger or sword? As it is written:

"For your sake we face death all day long;
we are considered as sheep to be slaughtered."

No, in all these things we are more than conquerors through him who loved us. For I am convinced that neither death nor life, neither angels nor demons, neither the present nor the future, nor any powers, neither height nor depth, nor anything else in all creation, will be able to separate us from the love of God that is in Christ Jesus our Lord.

—ROMANS 8:31–39

Those who are dominated by the sinful nature think about sinful things, but those who are controlled by the Holy Spirit think about things that please the Spirit. So letting your sinful nature control your mind leads to death. But letting the Spirit control your mind leads to life and peace.

—ROMANS 8:5–6 NLT

"Keep this Book of the Law always on your lips; meditate on it day and night, so that you may be careful to do everything written in it. Then you will be prosperous and successful."

—JOSHUA 1:8

. . . whose delight is in the law of the LORD,

and who meditates on his law day and night.

—PSALM 1:2

Within your temple, O God,

we meditate on your unfailing love.

—PSALM 48:9

I will consider all your works

and meditate on all your mighty deeds.

—PSALM 77:12

Though rulers sit together and slander me,

your servant will meditate on your decrees.

—PSALM 119:23

Cause me to understand the way of your precepts,

that I may meditate on your wonderful deeds.

—PSALM 119:27

I remember the days of long ago;

I meditate on all your works

and consider what your hands have done.

—PSALM 143:5

They speak of the glorious splendor of your

majesty—

and I will meditate on your wonderful works.

—PSALM 145:5

PART 3: THE REFRAME PRINCIPLE

Reframe Your Mind, Restore Your Perspective

Trust in the LORD with all your heart,
>   and do not lean on your own understanding.
In all your ways acknowledge him,
>   and he will make straight your paths.

—PROVERBS 3:5–6 ESV

I want you to know, my dear brothers and sisters, that everything that has happened to me here has helped to spread the Good News. For everyone here, including the whole palace guard, knows that I am in chains because of Christ. And because of my imprisonment, most of the believers here have gained confidence and boldly speak God's message without fear.

—PHILIPPIANS 1:12–14 NLT

"My thoughts are not your thoughts,
>   neither are your ways my ways,"
declares the LORD.
"As the heavens are higher than the earth,
>   so are my ways higher than your ways
>   and my thoughts than your thoughts."

—ISAIAH 55:8–9

This is the day that the LORD has made;
>   let us rejoice and be glad in it.

—PSALM 118:24 ESV

PART 4: THE REJOICE PRINCIPLE

Revive Your Soul, Reclaim Your Life

Praise the LORD.
Give thanks to the LORD, for he is good;
   his love endures forever.

—PSALM 106:1

. . . while he himself went a day's journey into the wilderness. He came to a broom bush, sat down under it and prayed that he might die. "I have had enough, LORD," he said. "Take my life; I am no better than my ancestors."

—1 KINGS 19:4

Rejoice in the Lord always. I will say it again: Rejoice! Let your gentleness be evident to all. The Lord is near. Do not be anxious about anything, but in every situation, by prayer and petition, with thanksgiving, present your requests to God. And the peace of God, which transcends all understanding, will guard your hearts and your minds in Christ Jesus.

—PHILIPPIANS 4:4–7

The LORD said, "Go out and stand on the mountain in the presence of the LORD, for the LORD is about to pass by."
   Then a great and powerful wind tore the mountains apart and shattered the rocks before the LORD, but the LORD was not in the wind. After the wind there was an

earthquake, but the LORD was not in the earthquake.
After the earthquake came a fire, but the LORD was not
in the fire. And after the fire came a gentle whisper.

—1 KINGS 19:11–12

The LORD is righteous in all his ways
and faithful in all he does.
The LORD is near to all who call on him,
to all who call on him in truth.
He fulfills the desires of those who fear him;
he hears their cry and saves them.

—PSALM 145:17–19

"*Abba*, Father," he said, "everything is possible for you.
Take this cup from me. Yet not what I will, but what
you will."

—MARK 14:36

Humble yourselves, therefore, under God's mighty hand,
that he may lift you up in due time. Cast all your anxiety on him because he cares for you.

—1 PETER 5:6–7

Do not conform to the pattern of this world, but be
transformed by the renewing of your mind. Then you
will be able to test and approve what God's will is—his
good, pleasing and perfect will.

—ROMANS 12:2

Those who are dominated by the sinful nature think about sinful things, but those who are controlled by the Holy Spirit think about things that please the Spirit. So letting your sinful nature control your mind leads to death. But letting the Spirit control your mind leads to life and peace.

—ROMANS 8:5–6 NLT

Let us then approach God's throne of grace with confidence, so that we may receive mercy and find grace to help us in our time of need.

—HEBREWS 4:16

The crowd joined in the attack against Paul and Silas, and the magistrates ordered them to be stripped and beaten with rods. After they had been severely flogged, they were thrown into prison, and the jailer was commanded to guard them carefully. When he received these orders, he put them in the inner cell and fastened their feet in the stocks.

About midnight Paul and Silas were praying and singing hymns to God, and the other prisoners were listening to them. Suddenly there was such a violent earthquake that the foundations of the prison were shaken. At once all the prison doors flew open, and everyone's chains came loose.

—ACTS 16:22–26

I will continue to rejoice, for I know that through your prayers and God's provision of the Spirit of Jesus Christ what has happened to me will turn out for my deliverance. I eagerly expect and hope that I will in no way be ashamed, but will have sufficient courage so that now as always Christ will be exalted in my body, whether by life or by death. For to me, to live is Christ and to die is gain.

—PHILIPPIANS 1:18–21

Why, my soul, are you downcast?
    Why so disturbed within me?
Put your hope in God,
    for I will yet praise him,
    my Savior and my God.

—PSALM 42:5

Bless the LORD, O my soul;
And all that is within me,
Bless His holy name!
Bless the LORD, O my soul,
And forget not all His benefits.

—PSALM 103:1–2 NKJV

Praise the LORD!
Praise the LORD, O my soul!
While I live I will praise the LORD;
I will sing praises to my God while I have my being.

—PSALM 146:1–2 NKJV

By day the LORD directs his love,
    at night his song is with me—
    a prayer to the God of my life.

—PSALM 42:8

Praise the LORD, all his heavenly hosts,
    you his servants who do his will.
Praise the LORD, all his works
    everywhere in his dominion.
Praise the LORD, my soul.

—PSALM 103:21–22

Be alert and of sober mind. Your enemy the devil prowls
around like a roaring lion looking for someone to devour.

—1 PETER 5:8

ACKNOWLEDGMENTS

I'D LIKE TO EXPRESS MY DEEPEST GRATITUDE TO ALL MY friends who helped make this book possible.

Amy Groeschel, you are my best friend forever. Thank you for being "overboard for God" with me for three decades and counting.

Vince Antonucci, you are the best of the best of the best. I sincerely thank God for your friendship for all these years. Your passion, creativity, and love for this message is evident on every single page. Your gifts are rare and special. Thank you for sharing them with me to expand the reach of our ministry. I'm profoundly thankful for you.

Dudley Delffs, I'm grateful for your investment on this project. Your feedback, suggestions, and edits made a real difference.

Katherine Fedor, thank you for being the most passionate detail person alive on planet earth.

Webster Younce, Andy Rogers, Brian Phipps, Robin Schmitt, Curt Diepenhorst, Paul Fisher, Trinity McFadden, and the whole team at Zondervan, it's truly an honor to publish with you. You honor Jesus with the work that you do, and it shows.

Tom Winters, it's hard to believe how many books we've done together. You are a trusted friend and one ridiculously scrappy agent.

ACKNOWLEDGMENTS

Adrianne Manning, you are the book whisperer. Thank you for caring as much as I do about this message. You make our ministry reach so much broader and our lives so much better.

To you, the reader, thank you for taking the journey with me. Let's do this together. Grab those thoughts that are contrary to his truth. Replace the lies you believe with God's unchanging truth. Change your thinking. And let God change your life.

NOTES

1. "What Is CBT Psychology, and What Are Its Benefits?" *betterhelp.com* (August 7, 2020), *www.betterhelp.com/advice /psychologists/what-is-cbt-psychology-and-what-are-its-benefits*.
2. Jena E. Pincott, "Wicked Thoughts," *Psychology Today* (September 1, 2015; last updated June 10, 2016), *www .psychologytoday.com/us/articles/201509/wicked-thoughts*.
3. Emily Dreyfuss, "Want to Make a Lie Seem True? Say It Again. And Again. And Again," *Wired.com* (February 11, 2017), *www.wired.com/2017/02/dont-believe-lies-just-people-repeat*.
4. Dan, "A New Word Every 98 Minutes," *EngLangBlog* (May 9, 2009), *http://englishlangsfx.blogspot.com/2009/05/new-word -every-98-minutes.html*.
5. A. Wilke and R. Mata, "Cognitive Bias," in *Encyclopedia of Human Behavior*, 2nd ed., ed. V. S. Ramachandran (Burlington, MA: Academic Press, 2012), *www.sciencedirect.com/topics /neuroscience/cognitive-bias*.
6. Wei-chin Hwang, "Practicing Mental Strengthening," in *Culturally Adapting Psychotherapy for Asian Heritage Populations* (Burlington, MA: Academic Press, 2016), *www.sciencedirect.com /topics/psychology/cognitive-reframing*.
7. See *www.drleaf.com/pages/about-dr-leaf*.
8. Quoted in Megan Kelly, "How Prayer Changes the Brain and Body," *Renewing All Things* (June 9, 2015), *https://renewingallthings.com /how-prayer-changes-the-brain-and-body*.
9. Michael Liedke, "Neurophysiological Benefits of Worship," *Journal of Biblical Foundations of Faith and Learning* 3, no. 1 (2018): 5, *https://knowledge.e.southern.edu/cgi/viewcontent .cgi?article=1063&context=jbffl*.

10. Peter A. Boelens et al., "A Randomized Trial of the Effect of Prayer on Depression and Anxiety," *International Journal of Psychiatry in Medicine* 39, no. 4 (January 2009): 377–92, *www .researchgate.net/publication/43146858_A_Randomized_Trial _of_the_Effect_of_Prayer_on_Depression_and_Anxiety*. Cited in Liedke, "Neurophysiological Benefits of Worship," 6.

11. James W. Anderson and Paige A. Nunnelley, "Private Prayer Associations with Depression, Anxiety and Other Health Conditions: An Analytical Review of Clinical Studies," *Postgraduate Medicine* 128, no. 7 (July 2016): 635–41, *www.researchgate.net/publication/305630281_Private_prayer _associations_with_depression_anxiety_and_other_health _conditions_an_analytical_review_of_clinical_studies*. Cited in Liedke, "Neurophysiological Benefits of Worship," 6.

12. Karen L. Kuchan, "Prayer as Therapeutic Process toward Aliveness within a Spiritual Direction Relationship," *Journal of Religion and Health* 47, no. 2 (July 2008): 263–75, *www .researchgate.net/publication/23686585_Prayer_as_Therapeutic _Process_Toward_Aliveness_Within_a_Spiritual_Direction _Relationship*. Cited in Liedke, "Neurophysiological Benefits of Worship," 6.

Hope in the Dark
Believing God Is Good When Life Is Not

In the midst of great pain, we may wonder if God really cares about us. Pastor Craig Groeschel invites us to wrestle with our questions and doubts while honoring our faith and asking God to heal our unbelief. Rediscover faith in the character, power, and presence of God.

The Christian Atheist
Believing in God but Living as If He Doesn't Exist

Join bestselling author and pastor, Craig Groeschel as he unpacks his personal walk toward an authentic God-honoring life. Groeschel's frank and raw conversation about our Christian Atheist tendencies and habits is a convicting and life-changing read.

Liking Jesus
Intimacy and Contentment in a Selfie-Centered World

Keep your eyes fixed on Christ instead of glued to a screen. Craig Groeschel teaches how to break unmanageable digital dependency and regain control of your life. *Liking Jesus* is a guide to bringing a balance of spiritual depth and human engagement back to your life.

Soul Detox
Clean Living in a Contaminated World

Without even knowing it, people willingly inhale second-hand cultural toxins poisoning their relationship with God and stunting their spiritual growth. *Soul Detox* examines the toxins that assault us daily, including toxic influences, toxic emotions, and toxic behaviors, and offers spiritual intervention with ways to remain focused on God's holy standards.

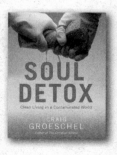

Fight
Winning the Battles That Matter Most

Fight helps uncover your true identity—a powerful man with a warrior's heart. With God's help, you'll find the strength to fight battles you know must be won: the ones that determine the state of your heart, quality of your marriage, and spiritual health of those you love most.

Divine Direction
Seven Decisions That Will Change Your Life

In this inspiring guidebook, bestselling author Craig Groeschel illustrates how the choices you make connect you to God and can lead you to a life you've only imagined. The achievable, disciplined, and simple steps in *Divine Direction* can take your life to wonderful and unexpected places only God could've planned.

Daily Power
365 Days of Fuel for Your Soul

Bestselling author Craig Groeschel's daily devotional will help you develop a consistent, daily pursuit of Jesus. In 365 brief devotions, Craig shares insights from his life that you can apply to almost every area of your own. *Daily Power* is here to help you grow and become strong every day of the year.

It Book with DVD
How Churches and Leaders Can Get It and Keep It

It. The life-changing, powerful force that draws people to you. What is *It* and how can you and your ministry get—and keep—*It*? Combining raw honesty with off-the-wall humor, this book explains how any believer can find *It*, get *It* back, and guard *It*.

Personal.
Practical.
Powerful.

CRAIG GROESCHEL
LEADERSHIP PODCAST

Subscribe to the **Craig Groeschel Leadership Podcast** on Apple Podcasts or wherever you listen to podcasts.

Visit **www.life.church/leadershippodcast** to find the episode videos, leader guides, discussion questions, and more.

 Apple Podcasts   Spotify

Google Podcasts   YouTube

Find practical leadership insights,
discover more books from Craig, and
see where Craig will be speaking next.

craiggroeschel.com.